ORIGAMI MODEL AIRPLANES

★ PATRICK WANG ★

TUTTLE PUBLISHING
Tokyo • Rutland, Vermont • Singapore

Published by Tuttle Publishing, an imprint of Periplus Editions (HK) Ltd., with editorial offices at 364 Innovation Drive, North Clarendon, Vermont 05759 U.S.A.

First published in Taiwan by Education Book Press Co., Ltd. 2005
Text and illustrations copyright © Education Book press Co., Ltd 2005. All rights reserved.
English language translation copyright © 2008 Tuttle Publishing

Library of Congress Control Number: 2008927792

ISBN 978-4-8053-0999-5

Distributed by

North America, Latin America & Europe
Tuttle Publishing
364 Innovation Drive
North Clarendon, VT 05759-9436 U.S.A.
Tel: 1 (802) 773-8930
Fax: 1 (802) 773-6993
info@tuttlepublishing.com
www.tuttlepublishing.com

Japan
Tuttle Publishing
Yaekari Building, 3rd Floor
5-4-12 Osaki
Shinagawa-ku
Tokyo 141 0032
Tel: (81) 3 5437-0171
Fax: (81) 3 5437-0755
tuttle-sales@gol.com

Asia Pacific
Berkeley Books Pte. Ltd.
61 Tai Seng Avenue #02-12
Singapore 534167
Tel: (65) 6280-1330
Fax: (65) 6280-6290
inquiries@periplus.com.sg
www.periplus.com

First edition
12 11 10 09 08   10 9 8 7 6 5 4 3 2 1

Printed in Singapore

TUTTLE PUBLISHING® is a registered trademark of Tuttle Publishing, a division of Periplus Editions (HK) Ltd.

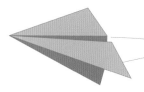

CONTENTS

3 Assembly Procedures of Airplanes

4 Works

Introduction of tools

Selecting suitable paper for origami

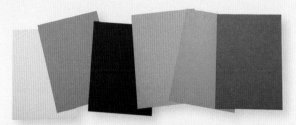

Cardstock paper

This kind of paper is thicker and harder, so it would be more difficult to use this kind of paper in small components. However, if you want to make an airplane in a large size, this kind of paper is thick and hard enough that the airplane won't look weak. Additionally, there are many colors to choose from.

Cardboard

Some parts in the airplanes need to be made using cardboard.

Letter-size paper

The thickness of this size paper is between the other two kinds, and is suitable for a regular size airplane. Additionally, there are many colors to choose from, or you can use white paper and paint on the colors you like. In this book, all of the procedures are depicted using letter-size paper.

Colored origami paper

This kind of paper is softer in material, brighter in color, and smaller in size. The airplanes made by this kind of paper may look weak, but this paper is good if you want to make a cute little airplane.

Tools

Scissors, Penknives

Pens, Rulers, Compasses, Erasers

Glue

You can use all kinds of glue, but since many airplanes need to be cohered to some components which are three-dimensional or standing, you'd better choose glue with good fixity. Here, we recommend white glue for paper airplanes, because white glue has a nice fixity after drying.

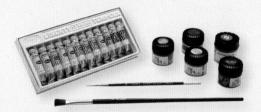

Pigments, Watercolors

Methods for Basic Components

There are two kinds of components—basic components and special components—in every airplane. We will introduce the methods for basic components in this chapter; for the special components, we will introduce them one by one in individual airplane chapters.

The scale

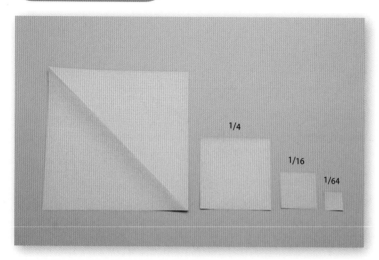

1/4

1/16

1/64

All of the papers for airplanes are with the same scale, so that the components would not be in different scales. In this book, for example, cut the letter paper into a square; we define it as size 1, then cut the square of size 1 into 4 squares; we define each as size 1/4, then cut the square of size 1/4 into 4 squares; we define each as size 1/16, then cut the square of size 1/16 into 4 squares; we define each as size 1/64. As shown in the figure, from left to right, are the squares of size 1, size 1/4, size 1/16, and size 1/64, respectively.

Basic component one: Kite

This component is the basis for all of the airplanes. For any airplane, more than 90 percent of the components will start with this, so become familiar with the folding method.

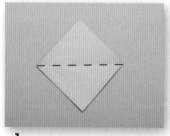

1 Use a square of size 1/4.

2 Valley fold in half into a triangle.

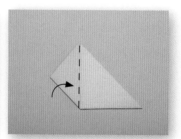

3 Valley fold the left corner to the center.

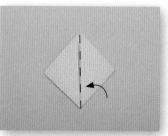

4 Valley fold the right corner to the center.

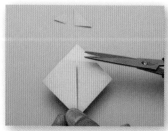

5 Cut off the two corners on the top layer for convenience in the later steps. The cut parts won't show up on the exterior.

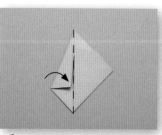

6 Valley fold the left edge to the center.

7 Valley fold

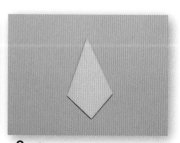

8 Flip over and it's done.

Basic component two: Rhombus

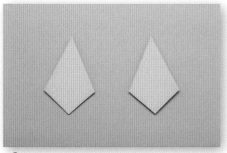

1 Start with two Kites.

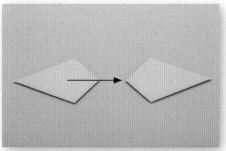

2 Flip over and place them face to face.

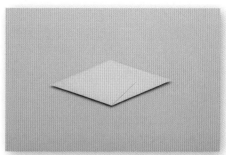

3 Use glue inside to glue the two parts to each other and it's done.

Basic component three

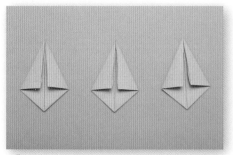

1 Start with three Kites.

2 Open one. Valley fold the right edge to the left crease.

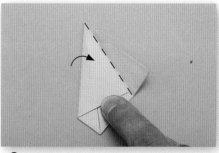

3 Take the second and open it. Valley fold the left edge to the right crease.

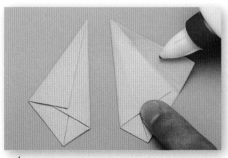

4 Use glue inside to cohere shape.

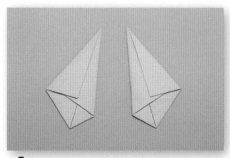

5 Place two parts side by side.

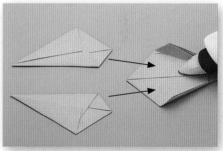

6 Let the completed two parts face the third and use glue inside.

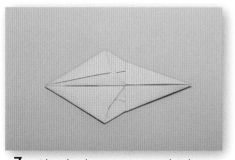

7 Glue the three parts to each other.

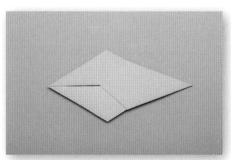

8 Flip over and it's done.

Basic component four: Horizontal stabilizer

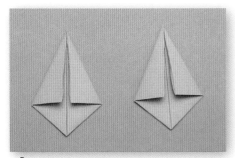

1 Start with two Kites.

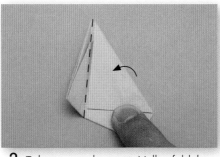

2 Take one and open it. Valley fold the right edge to the left crease.

3 Take the second and open it. Valley fold the left edge to the right crease.

4 Use glue inside. The procedure is the same for two parts.

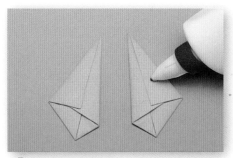

5 Use glue on one and glue the two parts to each other completely.

6 Done.

Basic component five

1 Start with a Kite.

2 Open it and valley fold the right edge to the left crease.

3 Open it again and valley fold the left edge to the right crease.

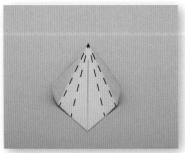

4 Open it again. There should be a total of four creases.

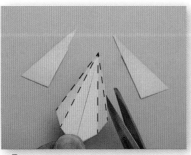

5 Cut along the outside two creases.

6 Valley fold along the inside two creases.

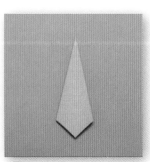

7 Flip over and it's done.

Basic component six: Half cone

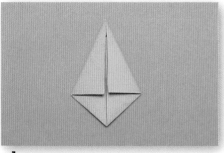

1 Start with a Kite.

2 Open it and fold up the bottom corner to the two creases.

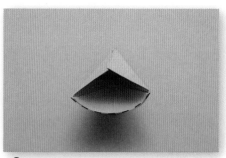

3 Curl the edge to a curve along the dashed line shown in the figure.

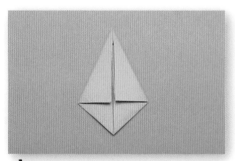

4 Use glue on one side.

5 Glue the two sides to each other.

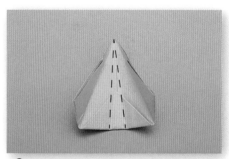

6 Flip over and it's done.

Basic component seven: Trapezoid-based pyramid

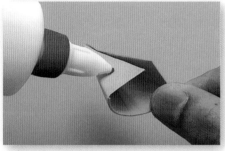

1 Start with a Kite.

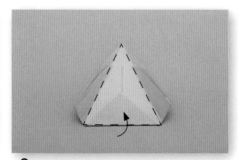

2 Open it and fold up the bottom corner to the two creases.

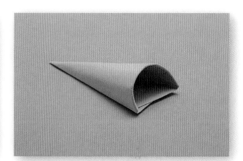

3 Make two creases near the center as shown in the figure.

4 Use glue on one side.

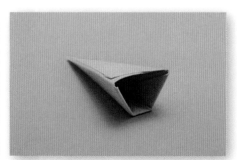

5 Glue two sides to each other.

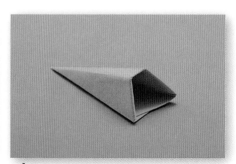

6 Flip over and it's done.

Basic component eight: Rectangular-based pyramid

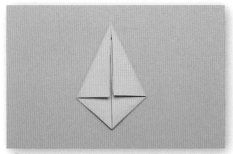

1 Start with a Kite.

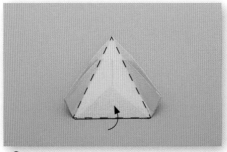

2 Open it and fold up the bottom corner to the two creases.

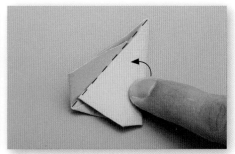

3 Valley fold the right edge to the left crease.

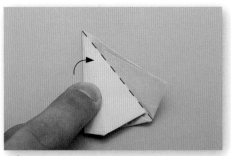

4 Similarly, open it and valley fold the left edge to the right crease.

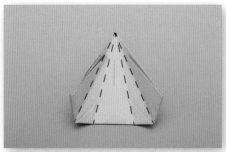

5 Open it again. There should be a total of four creases.

6 Use glue on one side.

7 Glue the two sides to each other.

8 Flip over and it's done.

Basic component nine: Nose

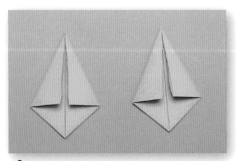

1 Start with two Kites.

2 Take one and flip over. Fold up the bottom corner.

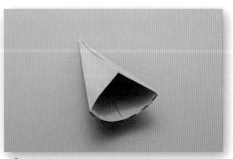

3 Flip over again. Curl the edge to a curve along the dashed line shown in the figure.

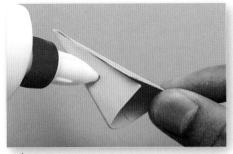

4 Use glue on one side.

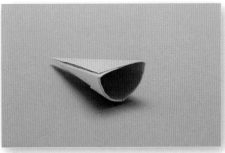

5 Glue the two sides to each other.

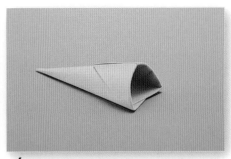

6 Flip over. The first part is complete.

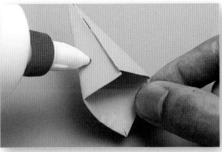

7 Take the other kite and curl the edge to a curve along the dashed line shown in the figure.

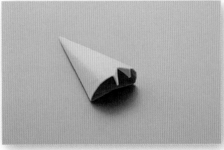

8 Use glue on one side.

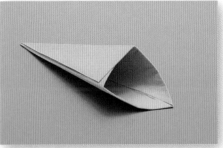

9 Glue the two sides to each other.

10 Flip over again. Cut a small gap along the center.

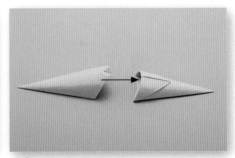

11 Fold down the two corners from the small gap.

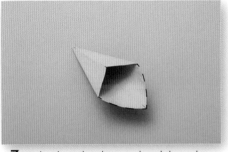

12 Place the two parts face to face.

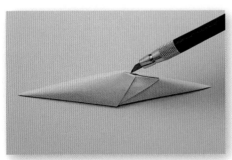

13 Tuck the two corners on the second part into the chink on the first part and use glue inside to fix tightly. You can use a sharp tool if it is difficult to tuck in.

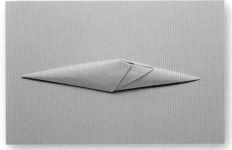

14 Done.

Basic component ten: Vertical stabilizer

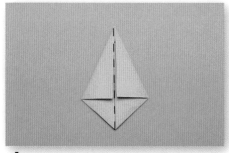

1 Start with a Kite.

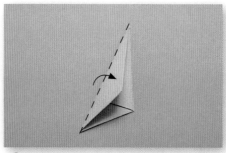

2 Valley fold in half along the center.

3 Inside reverse fold the top corner.

4 Cut along the edge to remove the protrusion.

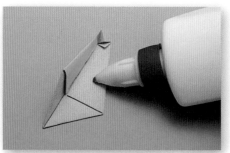

5 Use glue inside and cohere.

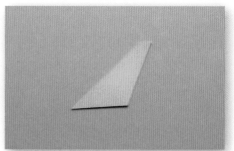

6 Done.

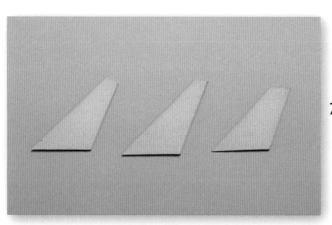

7 To make different airplanes, you can change the angle of the inside reverse fold to make different vertical stabilizers as shown in the figure.

Basic component eleven

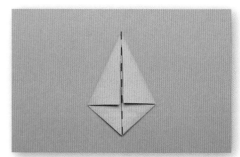

1 Use a square of size ¹/16 to make a Kite.

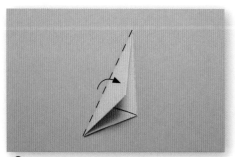

2 Valley fold in half along the center.

3 Use glue inside and cohere.

4 Done.

Basic component twelve

1 Use a square of size 1/16 to make a Kite.

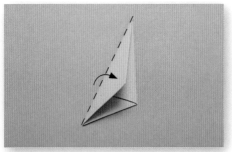

2 Valley fold in half along the center.

3 Use glue inside and cohere.

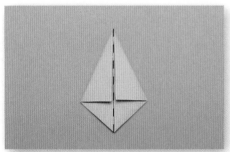

4 Cut it into three sections along the dashed lines shown in the figure.

5 After cutting, keep only the trapezoid of the middle section and discard the others.

6 Done.

Basic component thirteen

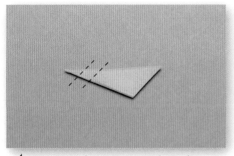

1 Use a square of size 1/16 to make a Kite.

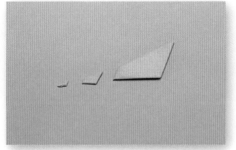

2 Valley fold in half along the center.

3 Use glue inside and cohere.

4 Cut it into two sections along the dashed line shown in the figure.

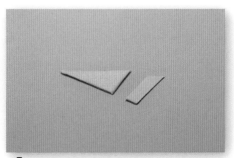

5 After cutting, keep only the trapezoid and discard the left section.

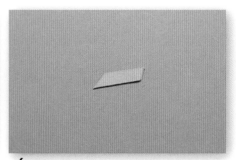

6 Done.

Basic component fourteen: Pylon

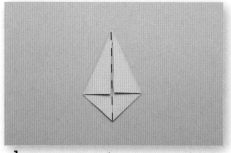

1 Use a square of size $^1/_{16}$ to make a Kite.

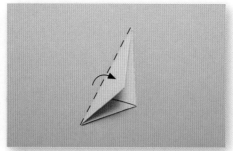

2 Valley fold in half along the center.

3 Use glue inside and cohere.

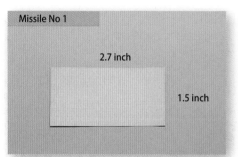

4 Cut it into two sections along the dashed line shown in the figure.

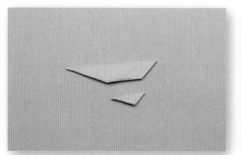

5 After cutting, keep only the trapezoid of the top section.

6 Done.

Basic component fifteen: Missile

Missile No 1

2.7 inch

1.5 inch

1 Use a 2.7 inch long, 1.5 inch wide rectangle.

2 Roll up into a cylinder.

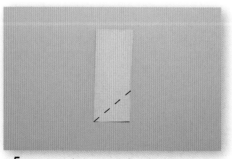

3 Use glue on the edge and cohere.

4 The body of the missile is complete.

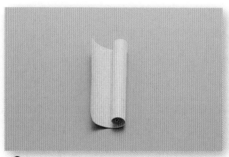

5 Use another rectangle of similar size.

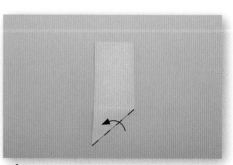

6 Fold up along the dashed line.

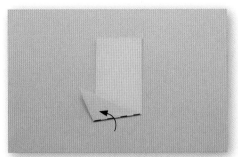

7 Fold up along the dashed line again.

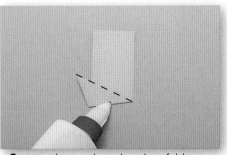

8 Use glue on the edge, then fold up along the dashed line.

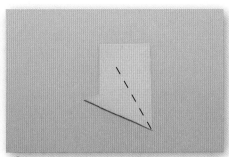

9 Cut along the dashed line.

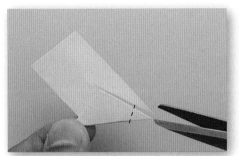

10 Cut off the small triangle along the dashed line.

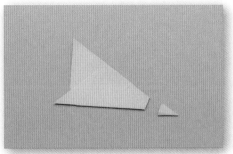

11 After cutting, keep only the small triangle.

12 Open up the triangle to make a cone.

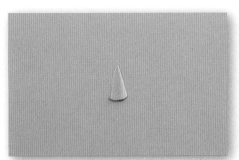

13 The warhead is complete.

0.4 inch

0.15 inch

14 Cut four rectangular cardboard pieces 0.4 inch long and 0.15 inch wide.

0.2 inch

0.15 inch

0.15 inch

15 Cut every rectangle into a triangle and a trapezoid as shown in the figure. The wings of the missile are now complete.

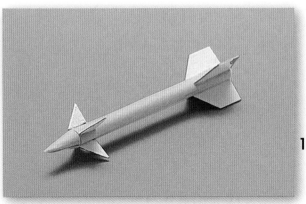

16 Glue the completed body, warhead, and wings together. The warhead is in front of the body and the wings are at four directions of the body. Missle no. 1 is complete.

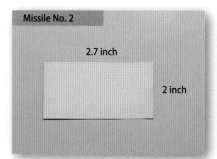

1 Use a 2.7 inch long, 2 inch wide rectangle.

2 Roll up into a cylinder.

3 Use glue on the edge and cohere.

4 The body of the missile is complete.

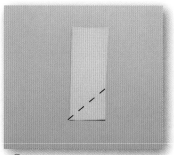

5 Use another rectangle of similar size.

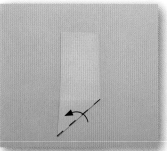

6 Fold up along the dashed line.

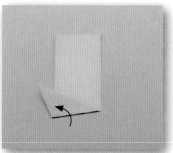

7 Fold up along the dashed line again.

8 Use glue on the edge, then fold up along the dashed line.

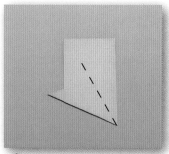

9 Cut along the dashed line.

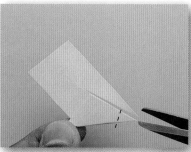

10 Cut off the small triangle along the dashed line.

11 After cutting, keep only the small triangle.

12 Open up the triangle to make a cone.

13 The warhead is complete.

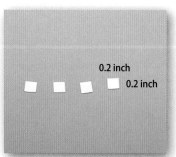

14 Cut four square cardboard pieces 0.2 inch long.

15 Cut every square into two triangles diagonally as shown in the figure. The wings of the missile are complete.

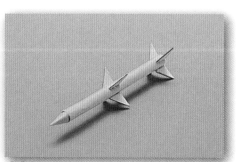

16 Glue the completed body, warhead, and wings together. The warhead is in front of the body and the wings are at four directions of the body. Missile no. 2 is complete.

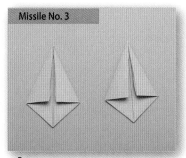

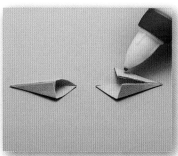

1 Use two squares of size 1/16 to make two Kites.

2 Use glue on one side and glue the two sides together. The procedure is the same for both parts.

3 Place the parts face to face.

4 Use glue on one part and glue the two together. The body of the missile is complete.

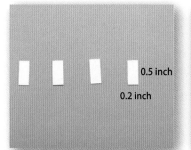

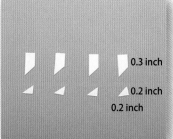

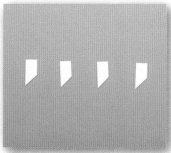

5 Cut four rectangular cardboard pieces 0.5 inch long and 0.2 inch wide.

6 Cut every rectangle into a triangle and a trapezoid as shown in the figure.

7 After cutting, keep only the trapezoid. The wings of the missile are complete.

8 Glue the completed body and wings together. Wings are at four directions of the body. Missle no. 3 is complete.

Basic component sixteen:
The combination of missile and pylon

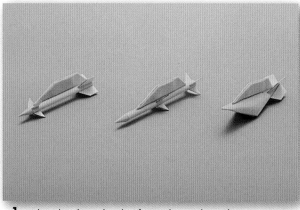

1 Glue the three kinds of Missiles to the Pylons, respectively, and we have three kinds of the combination of missile and pylon. As shown in the figure, from left to right, are the combinations of Missile no. 1 and Pylon, Missile no. 2 and Pylon, and Missile no. 3 and Pylon, respectively.

Basic component seventeen

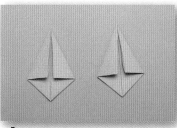

1 Use two squares of size 1/16 to make two Kites.

2 Use glue on one side and glue the two sides together. The procedure is the same for both parts.

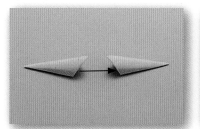

3 Place the two parts face to face.

4 Use glue on one and glue the two parts together. Done.

F-117
Nighthawk

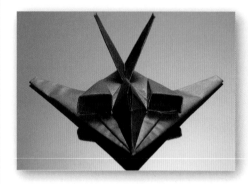

Level of difficulty ★☆☆☆☆

Specifications

Contractor: Lockheed Martin
Crew: 1
Length: 65 ft, 11 in
Wingspan: 43 ft, 4 in
Height: 12 ft, 5 in
Empty Weight: 30,000 lbs
Max. Takeoff Weight: 52,500 lbs
Speed: Mach 0.85

Component No.	Method
❶	Basic component nine: Nose
❷	Basic component eight: Rectangular-based pyramid
❸	Basic component two: Rhombus
❹	Special component: Wing, shown as follows
❺	Basic component four: Horizontal stabilizer
❻	Basic component ten: Vertical stabilizer

All of the components needed for assembling an F-117 Nighthawk are shown in the figure below.

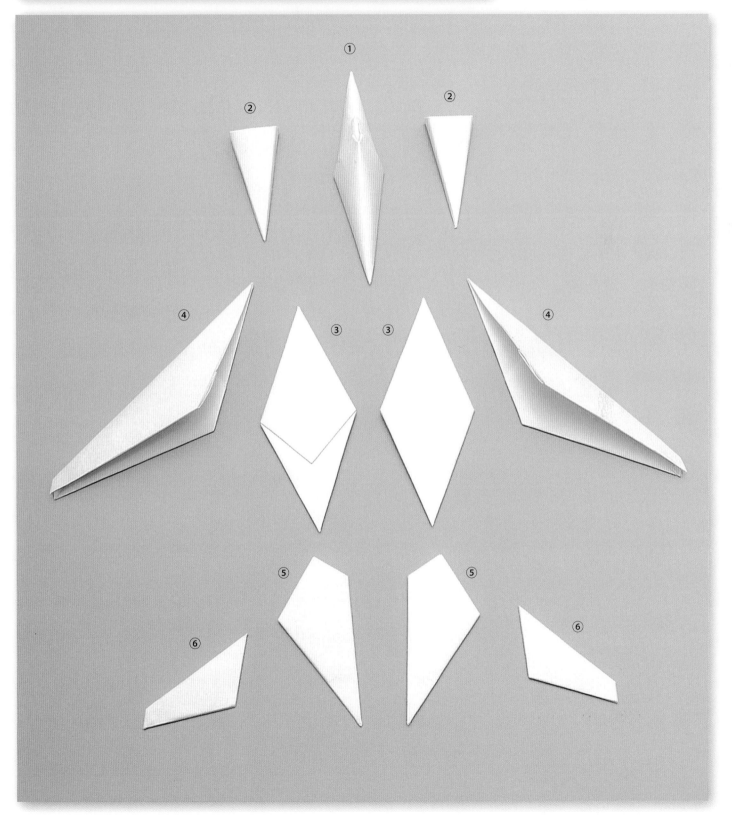

Methods for Special Components

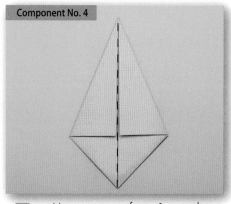

1 Use a square of size 1 to make a Kite.

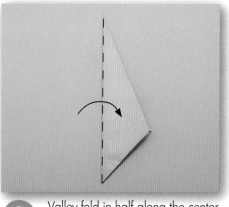

2 Valley fold in half along the center.

3 Inside reverse fold the top corner.

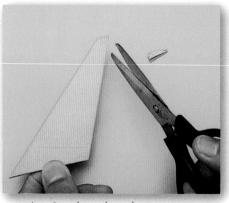

4 Cut along the edge to remove the protrusion.

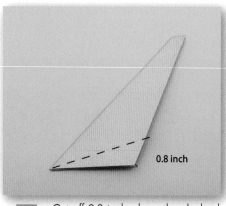

0.8 inch

5 Cut off 0.8 inch along the dashed line shown in figure.

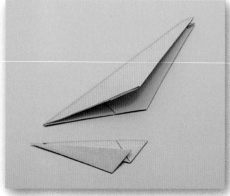

6 After cutting, keep only the top section and discard the bottom section.

7 Done. Repeat to make two wings.

Assembly Procedure

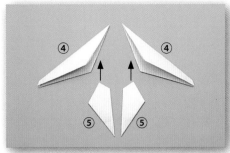

1 Use components no. 4 and 5 for the airframe.

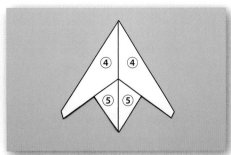

2 Glue two components no. 5 inside two components no. 4, respectively and place them next to each other as show in the figure.

3 Use one component no. 3.

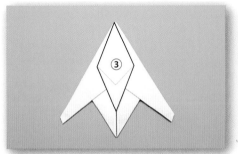

4 Glue component no. 3 on the top of the airframe.

5 Flip over and use the remaining component no. 3.

6 Glue component no. 3 to the airframe underbelly to match the top side.

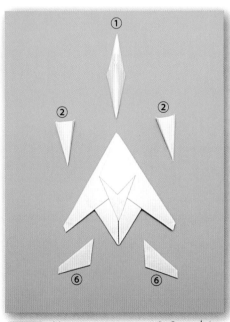

7 Use components no. 1, 2, and 6 for the top half.

8 Component no. 1 is the nose and is glued on front of the airframe. Two components no. 2 are air intakes and are glued on both sides of the nose. Two components no. 6 are vertical stabilizers and are glued to the rear of the airframe with an angle as shown in the figure.

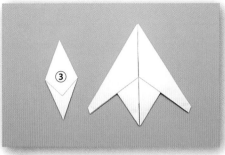

9 Reverse side.

10 Top view.

 F-117 Nighthawk **23**

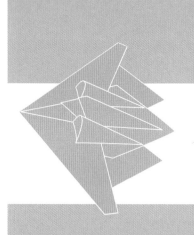

B-2
Spirit

Specifications

Contractor: Northrop Grumma
Crew: 2
Length: 69 ft
Wingspan: 172 ft
Height: 17 ft
Empty Weight: 162,000 lbs
Typical Takeoff Weight:
  336,500 lbs
Speed: 600 mph (Mach 0.8)

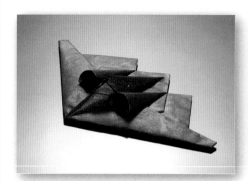

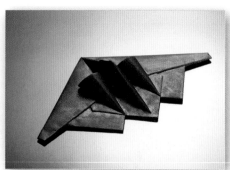

Component No.	Method
❶	Basic component nine: Nose
❷	Basic component six: Half cone
❸	Special component: Wing, shown as follows
❹	Special component: Airframe, shown as follows
❺	Special component: Airframe, shown as follows

All of the components needed for assembling a B-2 spirit are shown in the figure below.

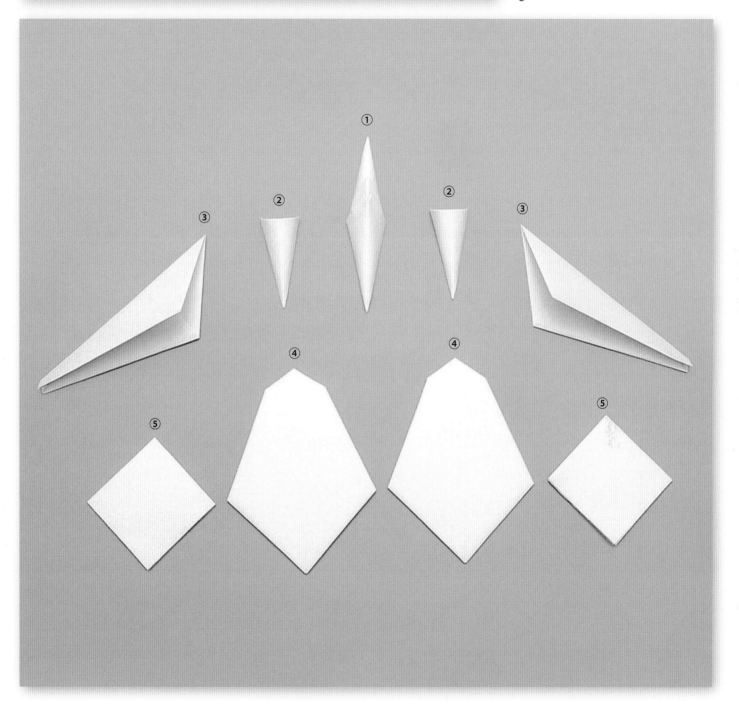

Methods for Special Components

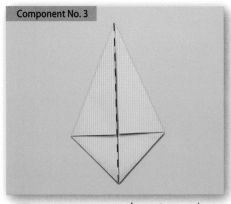

1 Use a square of size 1 to make a Kite.

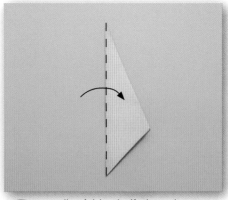

2 Valley fold in half along the center.

3 Inside reverse fold the top corner.

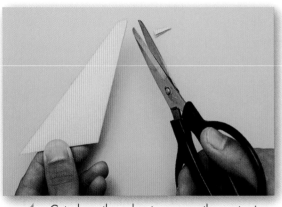

4 Cut along the edge to remove the protrusion.

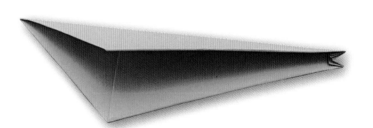

5 Done. Repeat to make two wings.

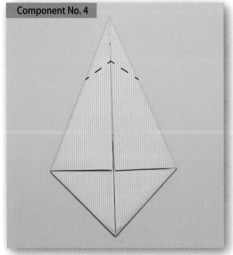

1 Use a square of size 1 to make a Kite and cut off the top corner along the dashed line shown in the figure.

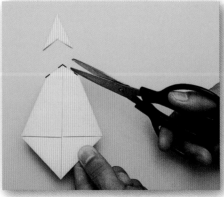

2 After cutting, keep only the bottom section.

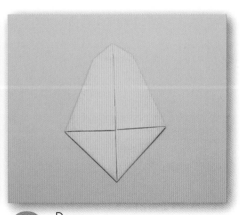

3 Done.

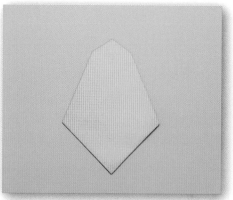

4 Flip over. Repeat to make two air frames.

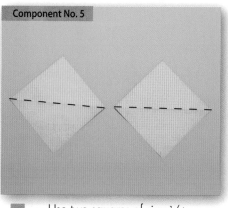

1 Use two squares of size 1/4.

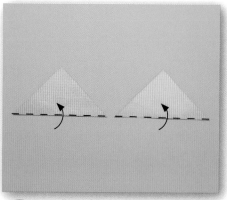

2 Valley fold in half into a triangle. The procedure is the same for the two components.

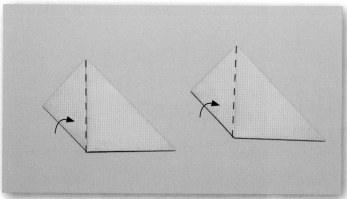

3 Valley fold the left corners to the center.

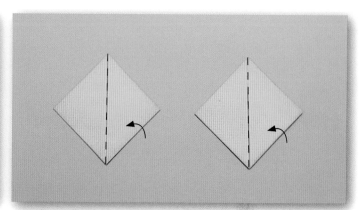

4 Valley fold the right corners to the center.

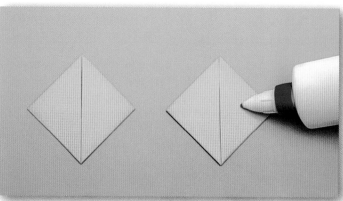

5 Use glue on one and glue them to each other completely.

6 Done. Repeat to make two airframes.

B-2 Spirit **27**

Assembly Procedure

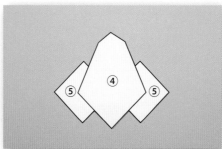

1 Use components no. 4 and 5 for the airframe.

2 Glue two components no. 5 to both sides of component no. 4 as shown in the figure.

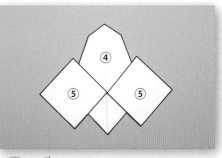

3 Flip over.

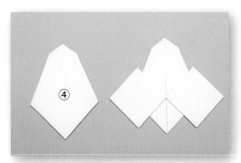

4 Then use the remaining component no. 4.

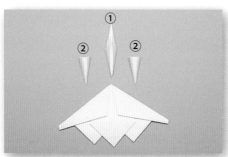

5 Glue component no. 4 to the airframe underbelly to match the top side.

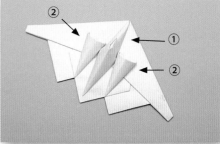

6 Use two components no. 3.

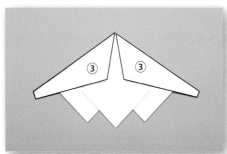

7 Place the completed airframe inbetween two components no. 3 and glue completely.

8 Use components no. 1 and 2 for the top half.

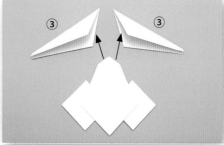

9 Component no. 1 is the nose and is glued on the center of the airframe. Two components no. 2 are air intakes and are glued on both sides of the nose as shown in the figure.

10 Reverse side.

11 Top view.

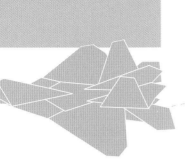

F-22
Raptor

Level of difficulty ★★☆☆☆

Specifications

Contractor: Lockheed Martin
Crew: 1
Length: 62 ft, 1 in
Wingspan: 44 ft, 6 in
Height: 16 ft, 5 in
Max. Takeoff Weight: 60,000 lbs
Speed: Mach 2

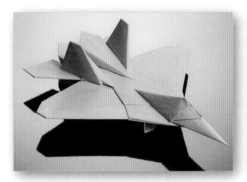

Component No.	Method
❶	Basic component nine: Nose
❷	Basic component three
❸	Basic component seven: Trapezoid-based pyramid
❹	Special component: Wing, shown as follows
❺	Basic component one: Kite
❻	Special component: Engine, shown as follows
❼	Basic component four: Horizontal stabilizer
❽	Special component: Vertical stabilizer, shown as follows

All of the components needed for assembling an F/A-22 Raptor are shown in the figure below.

Methods for Special Components

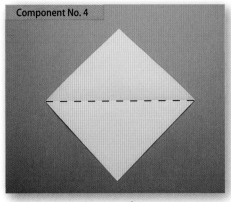

Component No. 4

1 Use a square of size 1.

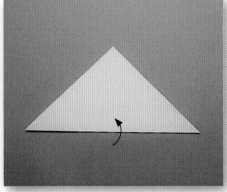

2 Valley fold in half into a triangle.

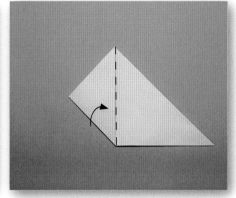

3 Valley fold the left corner to the center.

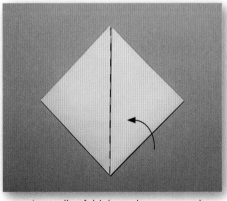

4 Valley fold the right corner to the center.

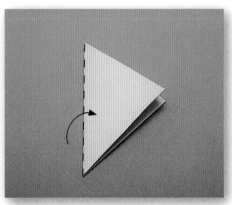

5 Valley fold in half along the center.

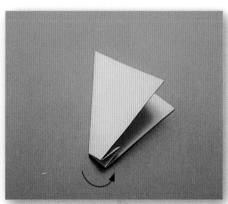

6 Inside reverse fold the bottom corner.

7 Cut along the dashed line shown in the figure.

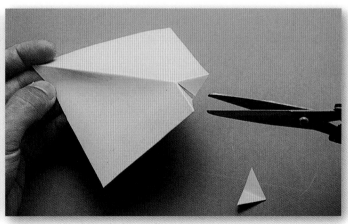

8 Cut along the central crease.

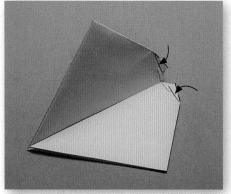

9 Inside fold the corners along the dashed line shown in the figure.

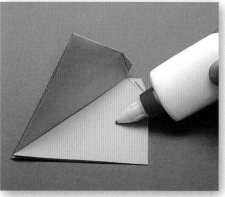

10 Use glue inside and cohere.

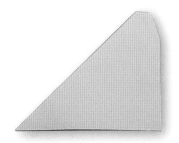

11 Done. Repeat to make two wings.

Component No. 6

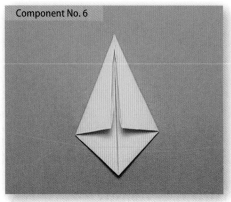

1 Start with a Kite.

2 Open it and valley fold the right edge to the left crease.

3 Similarly, open it and valley fold the left edge to the right crease.

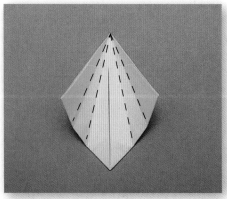

4 Open it again. There should be a total of four creases.

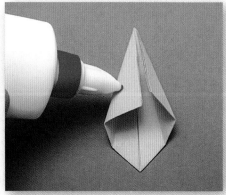

5 Use glue on one side.

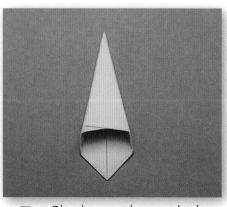

6 Glue the two sides to each other.

7 Flip over and it's done. Repeat three times to make four engines total.

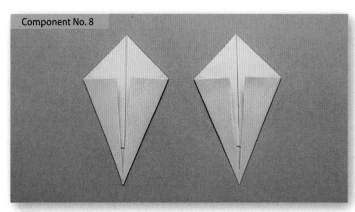

1 Start with two Kites.

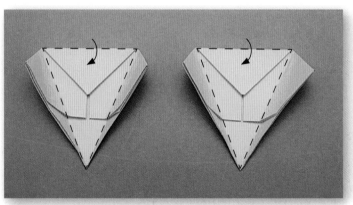

2 Open them and fold down the top corners to the creases. The procedure is the same for the two parts.

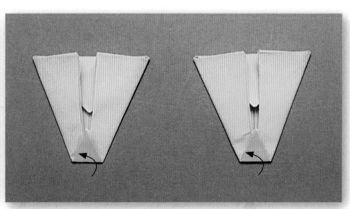

3 Fold up the bottom corners.

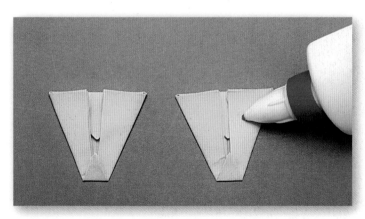

4 Use glue on one and glue the two parts to each other completely.

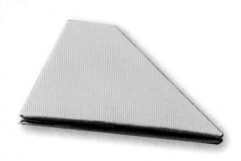

5 Done. Repeat to make two vertical stabilizers.

F-22 Raptor   **33**

Assembly Procedure

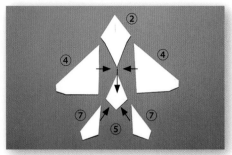

1 Use components no. 2, 4, 5, and 7 for the airframe.

2 Glue component no. 5 to the bottom of component no. 2, glue two components no. 4 on both sides, and glue two components no. 7 on both sides.

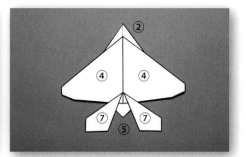

3 Flip over.

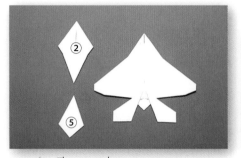

4 Then use the remaining components no. 2 and 5.

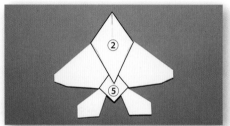

5 Glue components no. 2 and 5 to the airframe underbelly to match the top side.

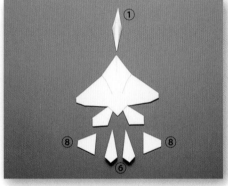

6 Use components no. 1, 6, and 8 for the top half.

7 Component no. 1 is the nose and is glued on front of the airframe. Two components no. 6 are engines and are glued to the rear of the airframe. Two components no. 8 are vertical stabilizers and are glued on both sides of the engines with an angle, as shown in the figure.

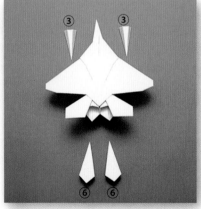

8 Then use components no. 3 and 6 for the bottom half.

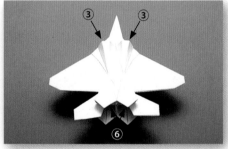

9 Two components no. 3 are air intakes and are glued on front of the airframe. Two components no. 6 are engines and are glued to the rear of the airframe as shown in the figure.

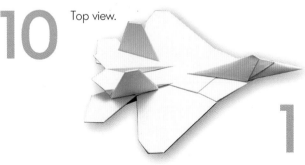

10 Top view.

11 Reverse side.

F-35

Specifications

Contractor: Lockheed Martin
Crew: 1
Length: 45 ft
Wingspan: 36 ft
Height: 14 ft
Empty Weight: 22,500 lbs
Max. Takeoff Weight: 50,000 lbs
Speed: Mach 1.6

Component No.	Method
❶	Basic component nine: Nose
❷	Basic component three
❸	Special component: Air intake, shown as follows
❹	Special component: Wing, shown as follows
❺	Basic component one: Kite
❻	Basic component six: Half cone
❼	Special component: Horizontal stabilizer, shown as follows
❽	Basic component ten: Vertical stabilizer

All of the components needed for assembling an F-35 Joint Strike Fighter are shown in the figure below .

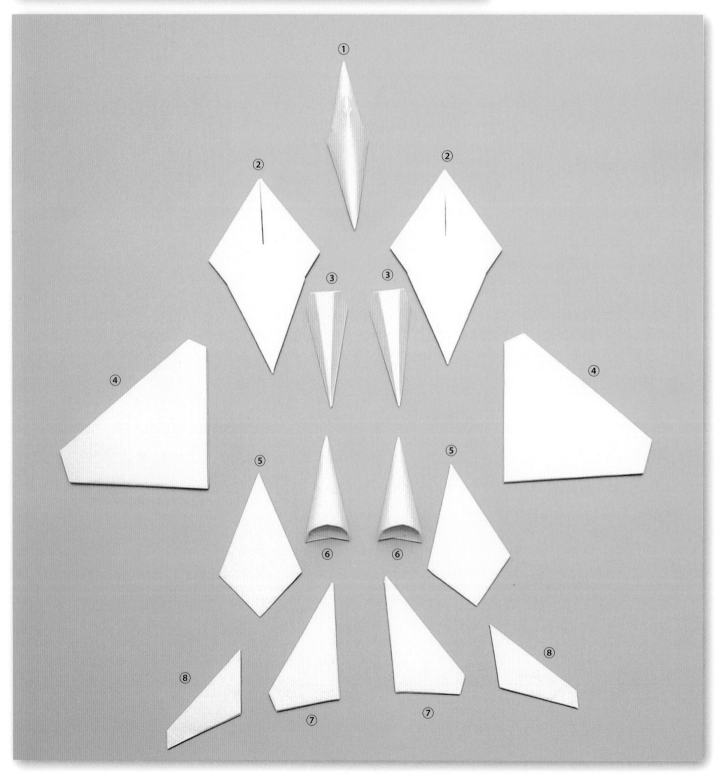

Methods for Special Components

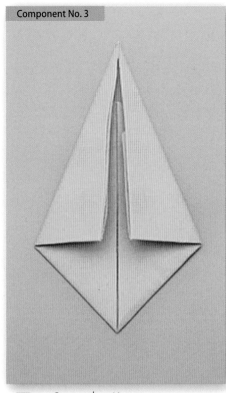

1 Start with a Kite.

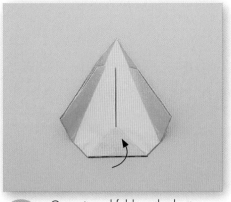

2 Open it and fold up the bottom corner along the dashed line.

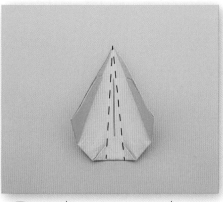

3 Make two creases near the center as shown in the figure.

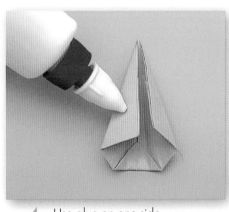

4 Use glue on one side.

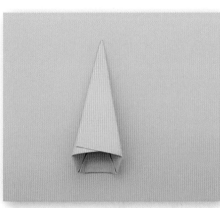

5 Glue the two sides to each other.

6 Flip over and it's done. Repeat to make two air intakes.

Component No. 4

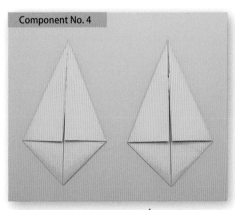

1 Use two squares of size 1 to make two Kites.

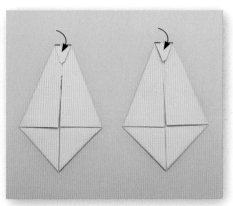

2 Fold down the top corners. The procedure is the same for the two parts.

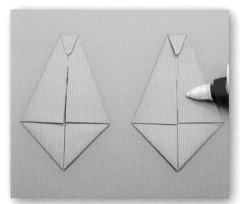

3 Use glue on one and glue the two parts to each other completely.

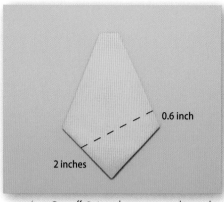

4 Cut off 0.6 inch on one side and 2 inches on the other side along the dashed line shown in the figure.

0.6 inch

2 inches

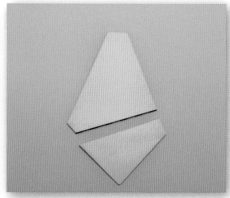

5 After cutting, keep only the top section and discard the bottom section.

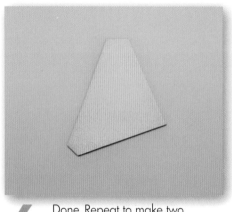

6 Done. Repeat to make two wings.

Component No. 7

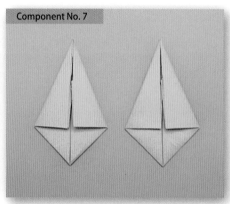

1 Start with two Kites.

2 Take one of them and open it. Valley fold the right edge to the left crease.

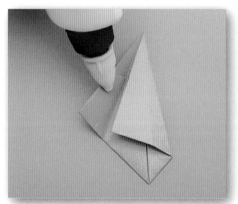

3 Use glue inside.

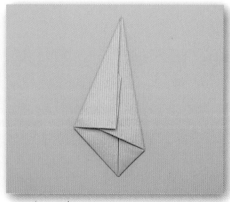

4 Cohere.

5 Fold up the bottom corner along the dashed line shown in the figure.

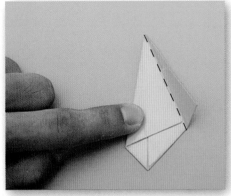

6 Similarly, take the other and open it. Valley fold the left edge to the right crease.

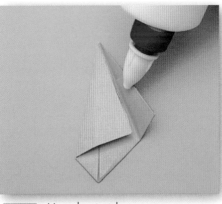

7 Use glue inside.

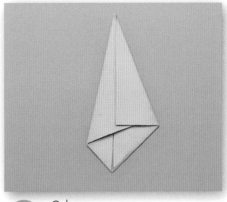

8 Cohere.

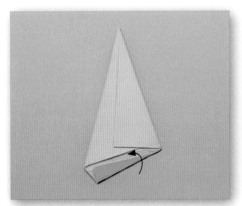

9 Fold up the bottom corner along the dashed line shown in the figure.

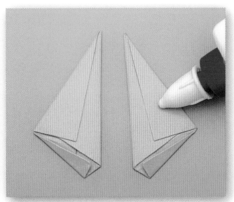

10 Use glue on one and glue the two parts to each other completely.

11 Done. Repeat to make two horizontal stabilizers.

Assembly Procedure

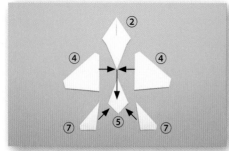

1 Use components no. 2, 4, 5, and 7 for the airframe.

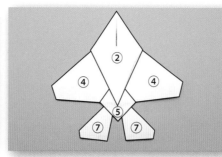

2 Glue component no. 5 to the bottom of component no. 2, glue two components no. 4 on both sides, and glue two components no. 7 on both sides.

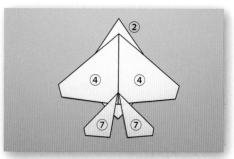

3 Flip over.

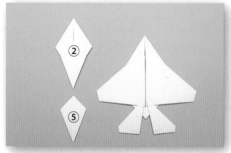

4 Then use the remaining components no. 2 and 5.

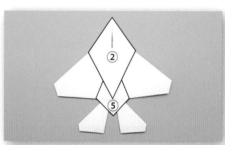

5 Glue components no. 2 and 5 to the airframe underbelly to match the top side.

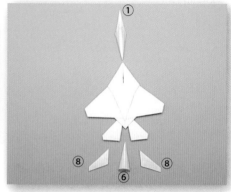

6 Use components no. 1, 6, and 8 for the top half.

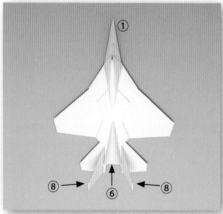

7 Component no. 1 is the nose and is glued on front of the airframe. Component no. 6 is the engine and is glued to the rear of the airframe. Two components no. 8 are vertical stabilizers and are glued on both sides of the engine with an angle as shown in the figure.

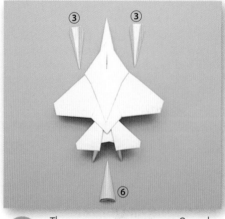

8 Then use components no. 3 and 6 for the bottom half.

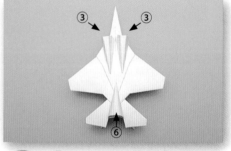

9 Two components no. 3 are air intakes and are glued on front of the airframe. Component no. 6 is the engine and is glued to the rear of the airframe as shown in the figure.

10 Reverse side.

11 Top view.

40 Origami Model Airplanes

P-47
Thunderbolt

Level of difficulty ★★☆☆☆

Specifications

Contractor: Republic
Crew: 1
Length: 36 ft
Wingspan: 41 ft
Height: 14 ft
Empty Weight: 10,700 lbs
Max. Takeoff Weight: 16,200 lbs
Speed: 430 mph
Range: 1,725 miles

Component No.	Method
1	Special component: Propeller, shown as follows
2	Special component: Fuselage, shown as follows
3	Use squares of size 1 to make Basic component five
4	Special component: Wing, shown as follows
5	Special component: Antenna, shown as follows
6	Special component: Vertical stabilizer, shown as follows
7	Special component: Horizontal stabilizer, shown as follows
8	Basic component sixteen: The combination of missile no. 3 and pylon

All of the components needed for assembling a P-47 Thunderbolt are shown in the figure below.

Methods for Special Components

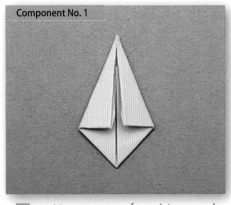

1 Use a square of size ¹/₁₆ to make a Kite.

2 Use glue on one side.

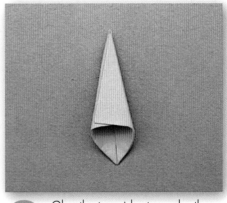

3 Glue the two sides to each other.

4 Flip over.

5 Cut two small chinks on the peak.

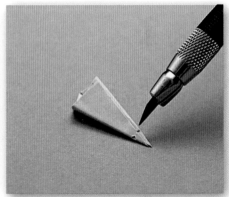

6 Similarly, cut two small chinks on the peak in the back side.

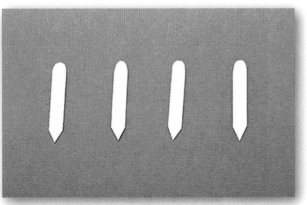

7 Then cut four propellers using cardboard as shown in the figure.

8 Use glue on the tips of the four propellers and cohere into the four chinks on the peak as shown in the figure and it's done.

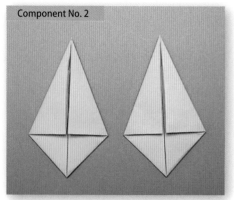

1 Use two squares of size 1 to make two Kites.

2 Take one of them and flip over. Fold up the bottom corner.

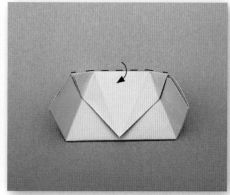

3 Flip over again and fold down the top corner.

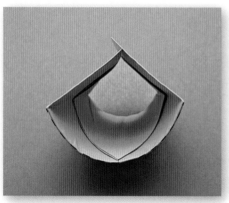

4 Curl the edge to a curve along the dashed line shown in the figure.

5 Use glue on one side.

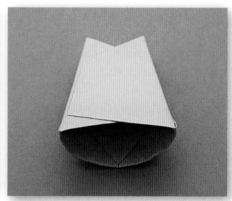

6 Glue the two sides to each other.

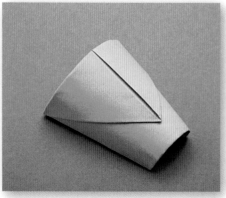

7 Flip over. The first part is complete.

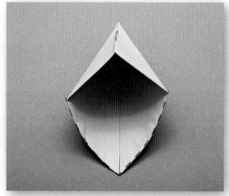

8 Use another and curl the edge to a curve along the dashed line shown in the figure.

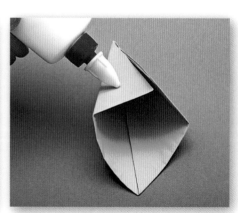

9 Use glue on one side.

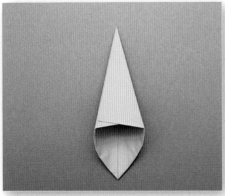

10 Glue the two sides to each other.

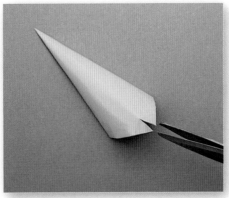

11 Flip over again. Cut a small gap along the center.

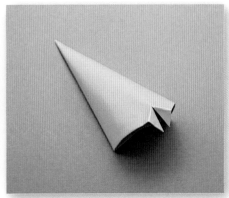

12 Fold down the two corners from the small gap.

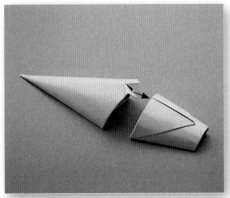

13 Place the two parts face to face.

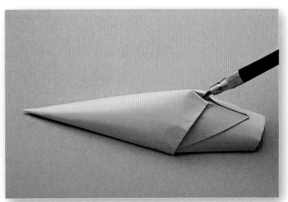

14 Tuck the two corners on the second part into the chink on the first part, and use glue inside to fix tightly. You can use a sharp tool if it is difficult to tuck in.

15 Done.

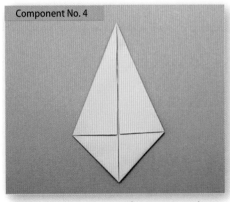

Component No. 4

1 Use a square of size 1 to make a Kite.

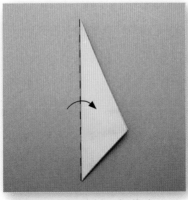

2 Valley fold in half along the center.

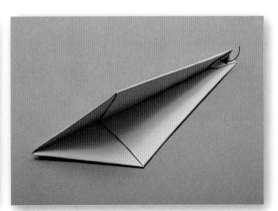

3 Inside reverse fold the top corner.

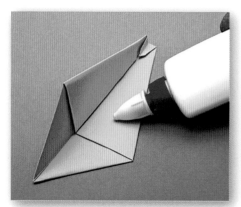

4 Use glue inside and cohere.

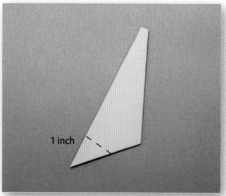

5 Cut off 1 inch on one side along the dashed line shown in the figure.

1 inch

6 After cutting, keep only the top section and discard the bottom section.

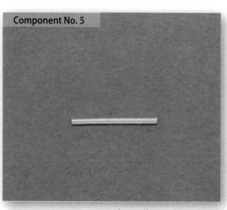

7 Done. Repeat to make two wings.

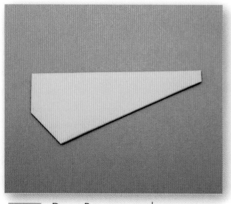

Component No. 5

1 Cut a piece of cardboard as shown in the figure.

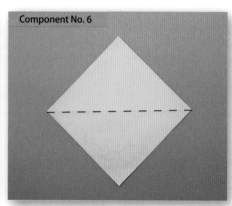

Component No. 6

1 Use a square of size 1/4.

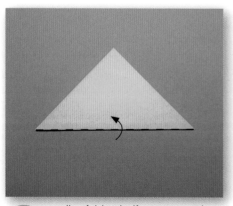

2 Valley fold in half into a triangle.

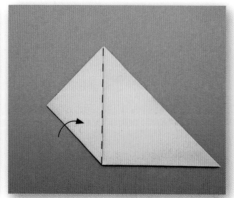

3 Valley fold the left corner to the center.

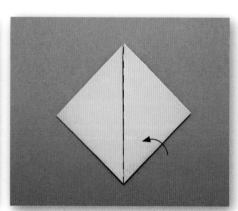

4 Valley fold the right corner to the center.

5 Cut off the two corners on the top layer for convenience in later steps.

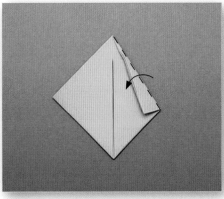

6 Valley fold the right side.

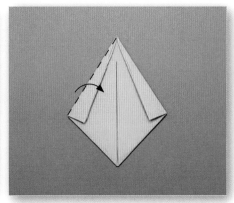

7 Valley fold the left side.

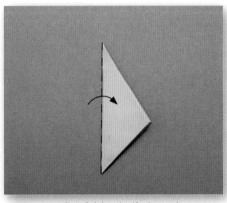

8 Valley fold in half along the center.

9 Inside reverse fold the top corner.

10 Cut along the edge to remove the protrusion.

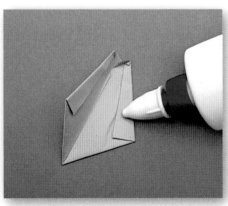

11 Use glue inside and cohere.

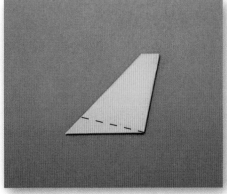

12 Cut along the dashed line shown in the figure.

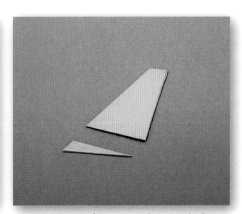

13 After cutting, keep only the top section and discard the bottom section.

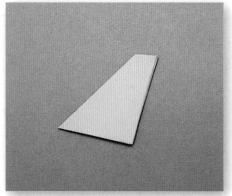

14 Done.

1 Start with a Kite.

2 Valley fold in half along the center.

3 Inside reverse fold the top corner.

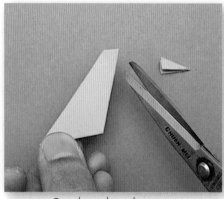

4 Cut along the edge to remove the protrusion.

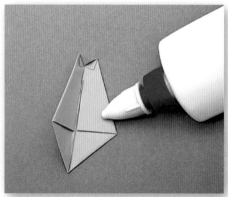

5 Use glue inside and cohere.

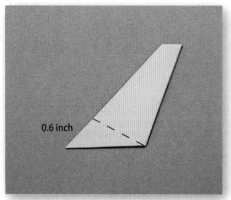

0.6 inch

6 Cut off 0.6 inch on one side along the dashed line shown in the figure.

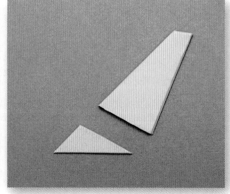

7 After cutting, keep only the top section and discard the bottom section.

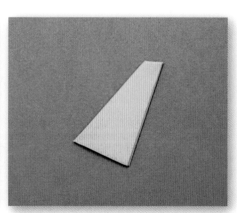

8 Done. Repeat to make two horizontal stabilizers.

Assembly Procedure

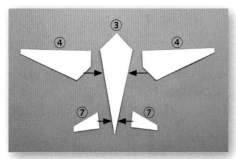

1 Use components no. 3, 4, and 7 for airframe.

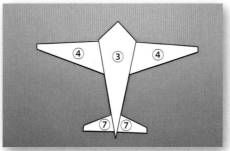

2 Glue two components no. 4 on both sides of component no. 3 for wings, and glue two components no. 7 on both sides for horizontal stabilizers as shown in the figure.

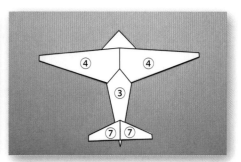

3 Flip over.

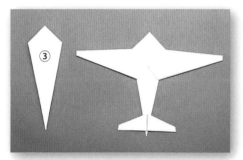

4 Then use the remaining component no. 3.

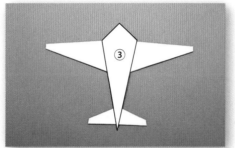

5 Glue component no. 3 to the airframe underbelly to match the top side.

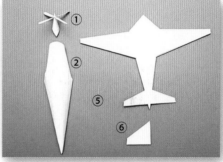

6 Use components no. 1, 2, 5, and 6 for the top half.

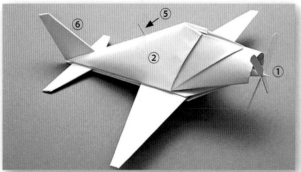

7 Component no. 2 is the fuselage and is glued on the airframe. Component no. 1 is the propeller and is glued into the hole of the fuselage. Component no. 5 is the antenna and is glued vertically on the fuselage. Component no. 6 is the vertical stabilizer and is glued vertically to the rear of the fuselage as shown in the figure.

8 Then use components no. 8 for the bottom half.

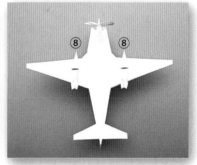

9 Components no. 8 are missiles and are glued vertically on wings as shown in the figure.

10 Reverse side.

11 Top view.

F-16
Fighting Falcon

Level of difficulty ★★★☆☆

Specifications

Contractor: Lockheed Martin
Crew: 1
Length: 49 ft, 5 in
Wingspan: 32 ft, 8 in
Height: 16 ft
Empty Weight: 19,100 lbs
Max. Takeoff Weight: 37,500 lbs
Speed: 1,500 mph (Mach 2)
Range: 2,400 miles

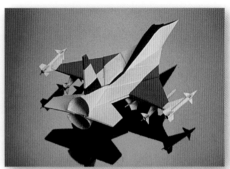

Component No.	Method
❶	Basic component nine: Nose
❷	Basic component three
❸	Basic component six: Half cone
❹	Special component: Wing, shown as follows
❺	Basic component one: Kite
❻	Special component, shown as follows
❼	Basic component four: Horizontal stabilizer
❽	Basic component ten: Vertical stabilizer
❾	Basic component fifteen: Missile no. 1
❿	Basic component sixteen: The combination of missile no. 2 and pylon
⓫	Basic component sixteen: The combination of missile no. 3 and pylon

All of the components needed for assembling an F-16 Fighting Falcon are shown in the figure below.

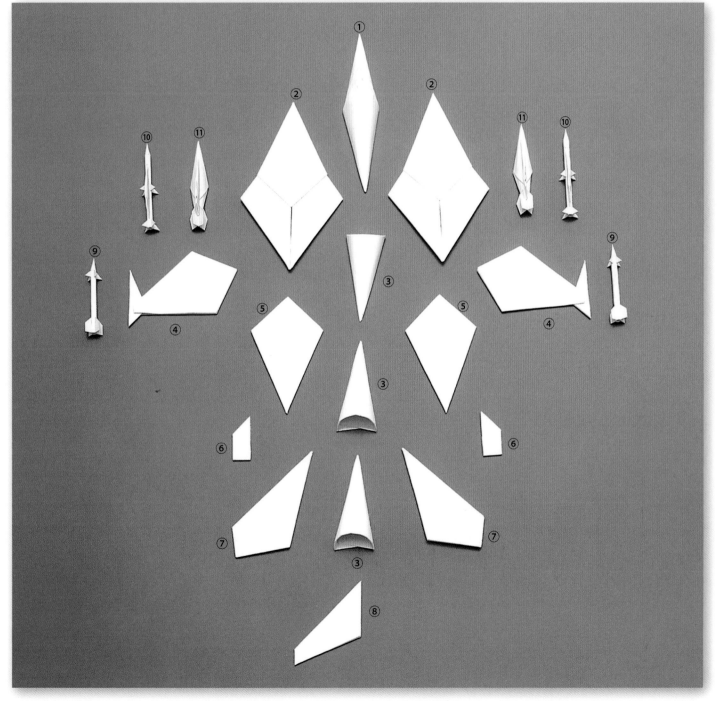

Methods for Special Components

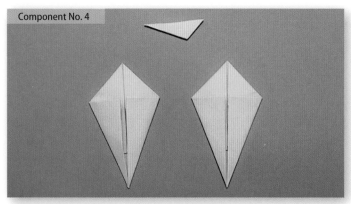

1 Start with two Kites and one Basic component eleven.

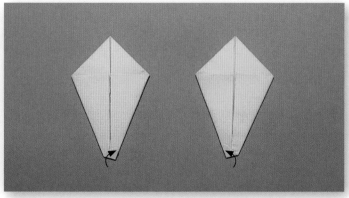

2 Take the Kites and fold up the bottom corners.

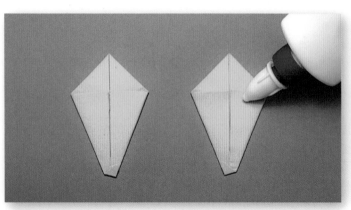

3 Use glue on one.

4 Glue the Basic component eleven between them as shown in the figure.

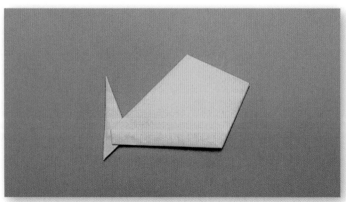

5 Done. Repeat to make two wings.

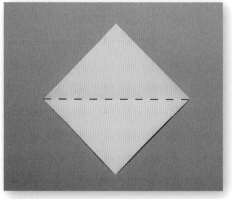

1 Use a square of size 1/16.

2 Valley fold in half into a triangle.

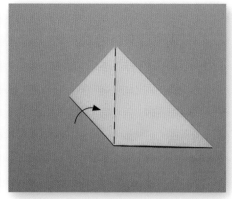

3 Valley fold the left corner to the center.

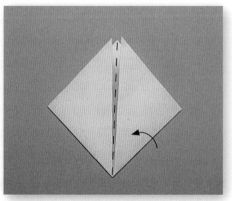

4 Valley fold the right corner to the center.

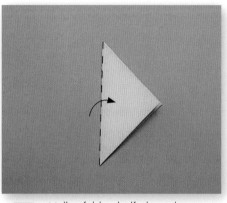

5 Valley fold in half along the center.

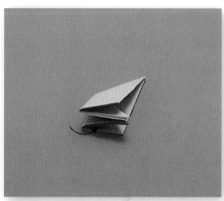

6 Inside reverse fold the bottom corner.

7 Cut off the protrusion.

8 Use glue inside and cohere.

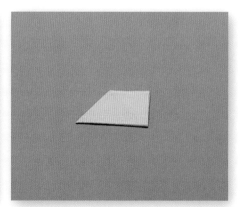

9 Done. Repeat to make two of these components.

Assembly Procedure

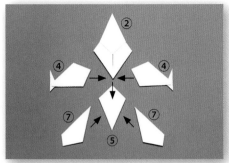

1 Use components no. 2, 4, 5, and 7 for airframe.

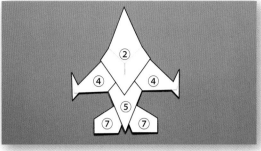

2 Glue component no. 5 to the bottom of component no. 2, glue two components no. 4 on both sides for wings, and glue two components no. 7 on both sides for horizontal stabilizers.

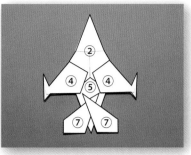

3 Flip over.

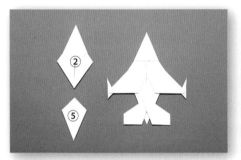

4 Then use the remaining components no. 2 and 5.

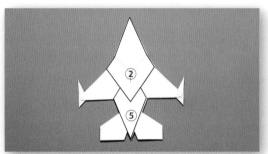

5 Glue components no. 2 and 5 to the airframe underbelly to match the top side.

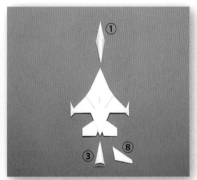

6 Use components no. 1, 3, and 8 for the top half.

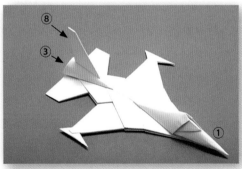

7 Component no. 1 is the nose and is glued on front of the airframe. Component no. 3 is the engine and is glued to the rear of the airframe. Component no. 8 is the vertical stabilizer and is glued vertically on the engine as shown in the figure.

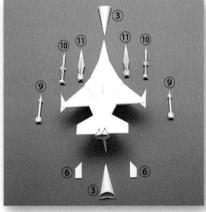

8 Then use components no. 3, 6, 9, 10, and 11 for the bottom half.

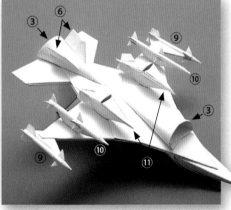

9 One of components no. 3 is the air intake and is glued on front of the airframe. Another component no. 3 is the engine and is glued to the rear of the airframe. Two components no. 6 are glued vertically on the engine, respectively. Two components no. 9 are missiles and are glued on both sides of wings. Components no. 10 and 11 are also missiles and are glued vertically on wings as shown in the figure.

10 Reverse side.

11 Top view.

F-14
Tomcat

Level of difficulty ★★★☆☆

Specifications

Contractor: Grumman
Crew: 2
Length: 61 ft, 9 in
Wingspan: 64 ft
Height: 16 ft
Empty Weight: 41,780 lbs
Max. Takeoff Weight: 72,900 lbs
Speed: Mach 2.3

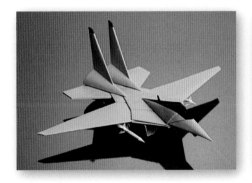

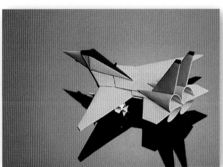

Component No.	Method
❶	Basic component nine: Nose
❷	Basic component twelve
❸	Use a square of size $1/64$ to make a "Basic component six: Half cone"
❹	Basic component three
❺	Special component Wing, shown as follows
❻	Basic component seven: Trapezoid-based pyramid
❼	Basic component one: Kite
❽	Basic component six: Half cone
❾	Basic component eleven
❿	Basic component four: Horizontal stabilizer
⓫	Basic component ten Vertical stabilizer
⓬	Special component Missile set, shown as follows

All of the components needed for assembling an F-14 Tomcat are shown in the figure below.

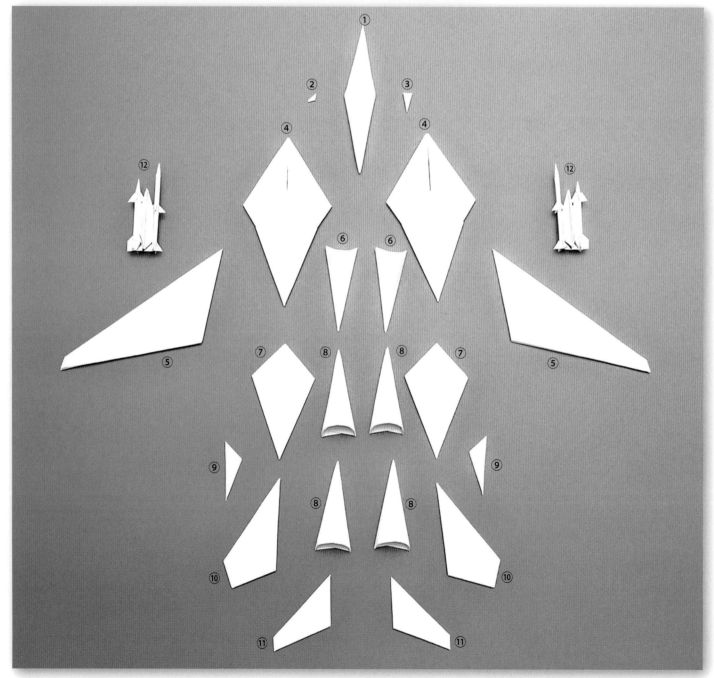

Methods for Special Components

1 Use a square of size 1 to make a Kite.

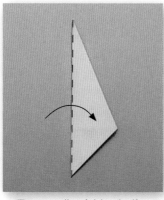

2 Valley fold in half along the center.

3 Inside reverse fold the top corner.

4 Cut along the edge to remove the protrusion.

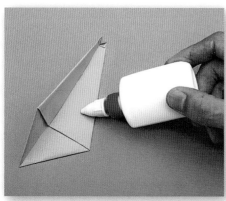

5 Use glue inside and cohere.

6 Done. Repeat to make two wings.

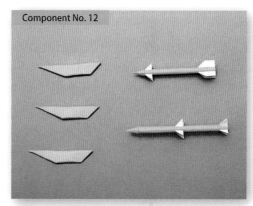

Component No. 12

1 Start with three Pylons, one Missile No. 1, and one Missile No. 2.

2 Take the three Pylons and place glue on the edge of every Pylon, so that you can glue them vertically as shown in the figure.

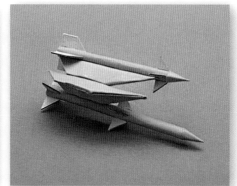

3 Glue two missiles on the edge of the pylon. Missile no. 1 is glued on the side and missile no. 2 is glued on the bottom as shown in the figure.

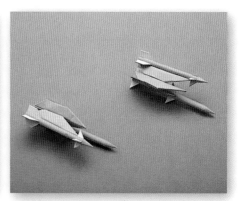

4 Repeat to make two missile sets, but notice that, the direction of these two missile sets is symmetrical.

Assembly Procedure

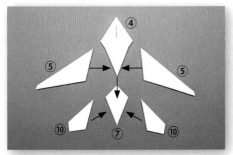

1 Use components no. 4, 5, 7, and 10, for airframe.

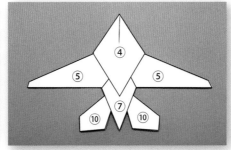

2 Glue component no. 7 to the bottom of component no. 4, glue two components no. 5 on both sides, and glue two components no. 10 on both sides.

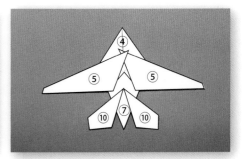

3 Flip over.

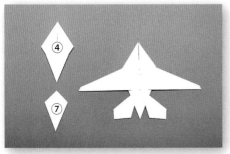

4 Then use the remaining components no. 4 and 7.

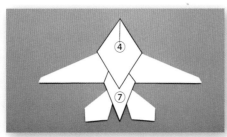

5 Glue components no. 4 and 7 to the airframe underbelly to match the top side.

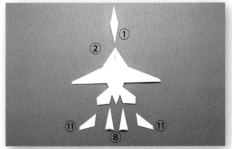

6 Use components no. 1, 2, 8, and 11 for the top half.

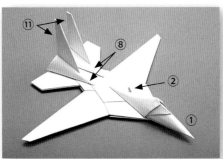

7 Component no. 1 is glued on front of the airframe. Component no. 2 is glued on the nose vertically. Two components no. 8 are glued to the rear of the airframe. Two components no. 11 and are glued vertically on engines.

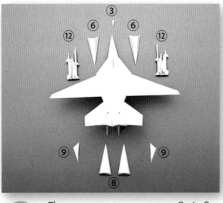

8 Then use components no. 3, 6, 8, 9, and 12 for the bottom half.

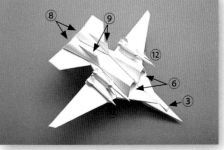

9 Component no. 3 is glued on the nose. Two components no. 6 are air intakes and are glued on front of the airframe. Two components no. 8 are engines and are glued to the rear of the airframe. Two components no. 9 are glued on the engines vertically. Two components no. 12 are missile sets and are glued on wings as shown in the figure.

10 Reverse side.

11 Top view.

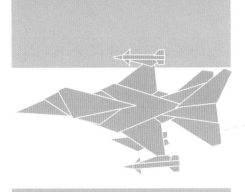

IDF

經國

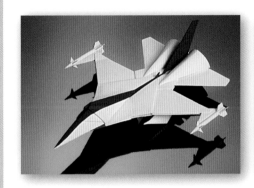

Level of difficulty ★★★☆☆

Specifications

Contractor: AIDC (Taiwan)
Crew: 1
Length: 43 ft, 6 in
Wingspan: 29 ft, 6 in
Height: 13 ft, 3 in
Empty Weight: 20,000 lbs
Max. Takeoff Weight: 27,000 lbs
Speed: 800 mph

Component No.	Method
❶	Basic component nine: Nose
❷	Basic component three
❸	Special component: Wing, shown as follows
❹	Basic component six: Half cone
❺	Basic component one: Kite
❻	Special component: Horizontal stabilizer, shown as follows
❼	Basic component twelve
❽	Basic component ten: Vertical stabilizer
❾	Basic component fifteen: Missile no. 1
❿	Basic component sixteen: The combination of missile no. 3 and pylon

All of the components needed for assembling an IDF Ching Kuo are shown in the figure below.

Methods for Special Components

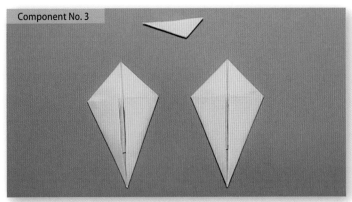

1 Start with two Kites and one Basic component eleven.

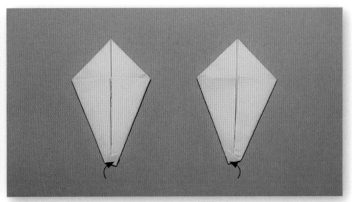

2 Take the two Kites and fold up the bottom corners.

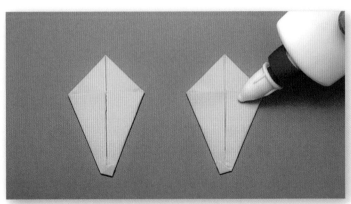

3 Use glue on one part.

4 Glue the Basic component eleven between them as shown in the figure.

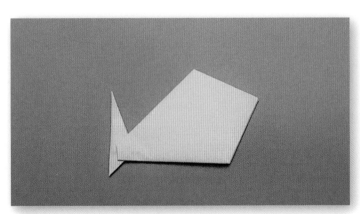

5 Done. Repeat to make two wings.

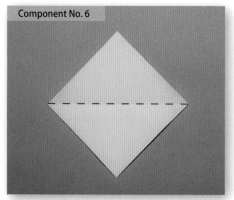

1 Use a square of size 1/4.

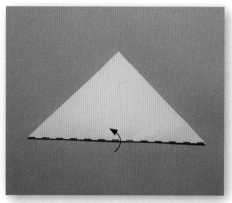

2 Valley fold in half into a triangle.

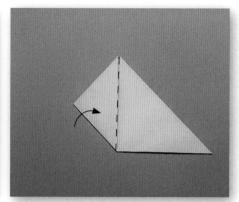

3 Valley fold the left corner to the center.

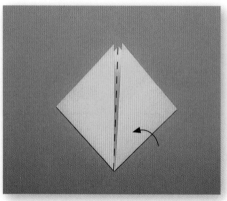

4 Valley fold the right corner to the center.

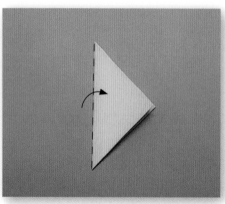

5 Valley fold in half along the center.

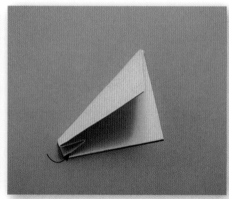

6 Inside reverse fold the bottom corner.

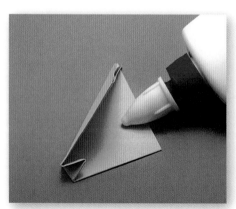

7 Use glue inside and cohere.

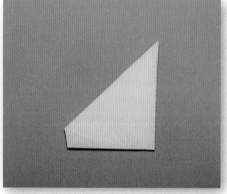

8 Done. Repeat to make two horizontal stabilizers.

Assembly Procedure

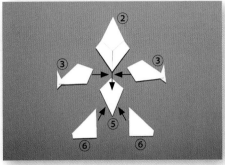

1 Use components no. 2, 3, 5, and 6 for airframe.

2 Glue component no. 5 to the bottom of component no. 2, glue two components no. 3 on both sides for wings, and glue two components no. 6 on both sides for horizontal stabilizers as shown in the figure.

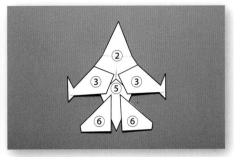

3 Flip over.

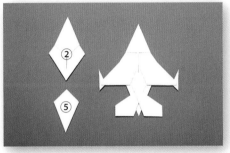

4 Then use the remaining components no. 2 and 5.

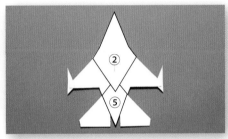

5 Glue components no. 2 and 5 to the airframe underbelly to match the top side.

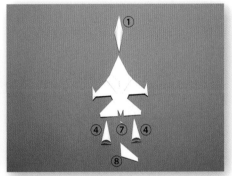

6 Use components no. 1, 4, 7, and 8 for the top half.

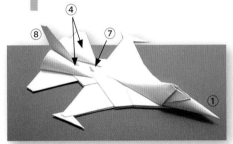

7 Component no. 1 is the nose and is glued on front of the airframe. Two components no. 4 are engines and are glued to the rear of the airframe. Component no. 7 is glued vertically to the center of the airframe. Component no. 8 is the vertical stabilizer and is glued vertically between the two engines as shown in the figure.

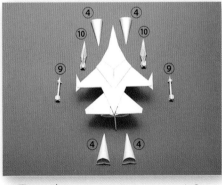

8 Then use components no. 4, 9, and 10 for the bottom half.

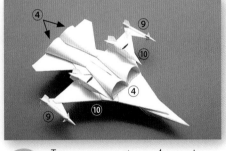

9 Two components no. 4 are air intakes and are glued on front of the airframe. The other two components no. 4 are engines and are glued to the rear of the airframe. Two components no. 9 are missiles and are glued on both sides of wings. Two components no. 10 are also missiles and are glued vertically on wings as shown in the figure.

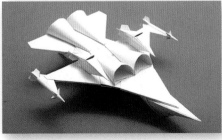

10 Reverse side.

11 Top view.

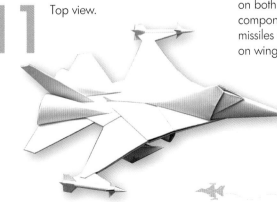

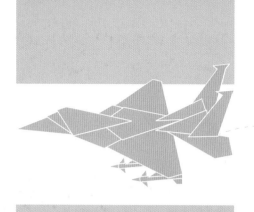

F-15
Eagle

Level of difficulty ★★★☆☆

Specifications

Contractor: McDonnell Douglas
Crew: 1
Length: 63.8 ft
Wingspan: 42.8 ft
Height: 18.5 ft
Empty Weight: 28,600 lbs
Max. Takeoff Weight: 68,000 lbs
Speed: 1,880 mph (Mach 2.5)
Range: 3,450 miles

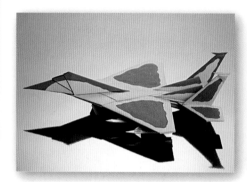

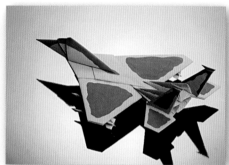

Component No.	Method
❶	Basic component nine: Nose
❷	Basic component three
❸	Basic component seven: Trapezoid-based pyramid
❹	Special component: Wing, shown as follows
❺	Basic component one: Kite
❻	Basic component six: Half cone
❼	Basic component four: Horizontal stabilizer
❽	Special component: Vertical stabilizer, shown as follows
❾	Basic component sixteen: The combination of missile no. 1 and pylon
❿	Basic component sixteen: The combination of missile no. 2 and pylon
⓫	Basic component sixteen: The combination of missile no. 3 and pylon

All of the components needed for assembling an F-15 Eagle are shown in the figure below.

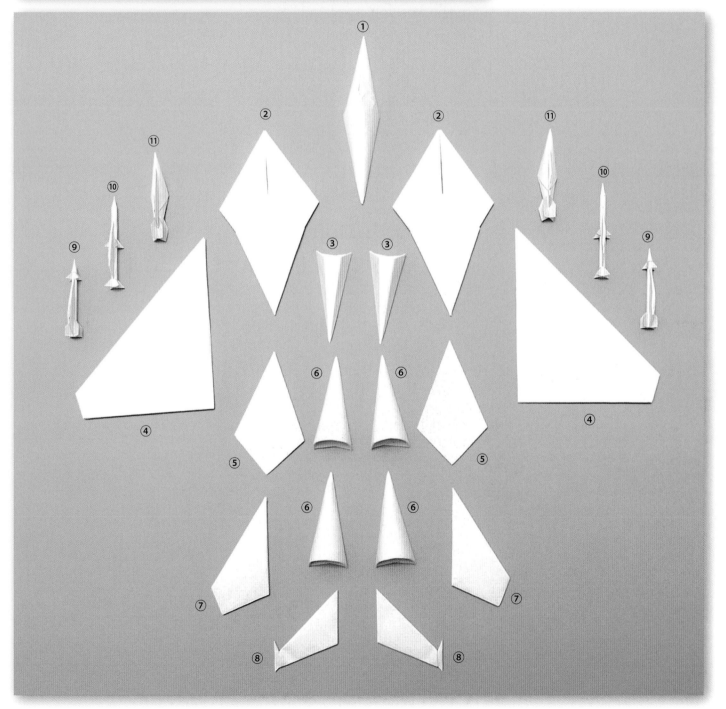

Methods for Special Components

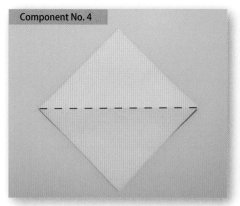

1 Use a square of size 1.

2 Valley fold in half into a triangle.

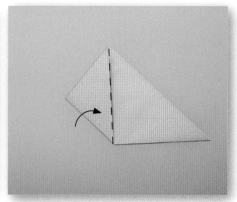

3 Valley fold the left corner to the center.

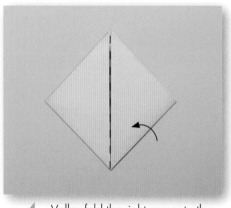

4 Valley fold the right corner to the center.

5 Valley fold in half along the center.

6 Inside reverse fold the bottom corner.

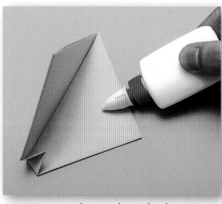

7 Use glue inside and cohere.

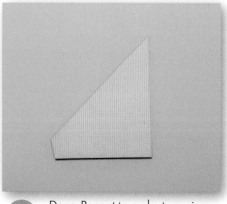

8 Done. Repeat to make two wings.

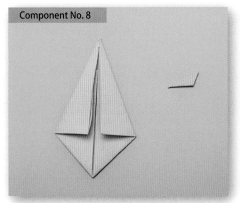

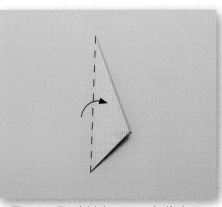

1 Start with a Kite and use a square of size $1/64$ to make a Basic component eleven.

2 Valley fold the Kite in half along the center.

3 Inside reverse fold the top corner.

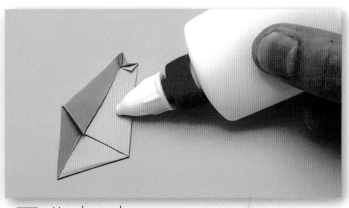

4 Cut along the edge to remove the protrusion.

5 Use glue inside.

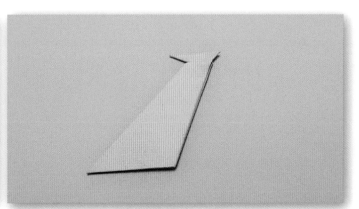

6 Glue the Basic component eleven inside the top section.

7 Done. Repeat to make two vertical stabilizers.

Assembly Procedure

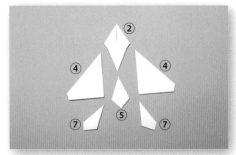

1 Use components no. 2, 4, 5, and 7 for airframe.

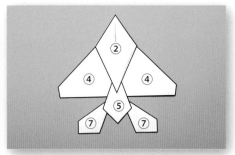

2 Glue component no. 5 to the bottom of component no. 2, glue two components no. 4 on both sides for wings, and glue two components no. 7 on both sides for horizontal stabilizers.

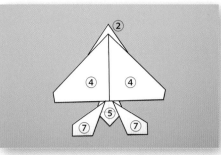

3 Flip over.

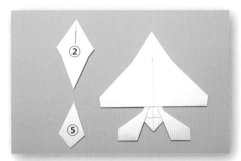

4 Then use the remaining components no. 2 and 5.

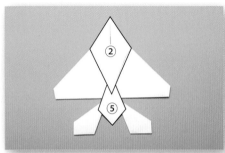

5 Glue components no. 2 and 5 to the airframe underbelly to match the top side.

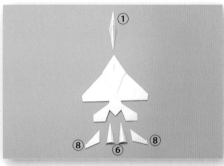

6 Use components no. 1, 6, and 8 for the top half.

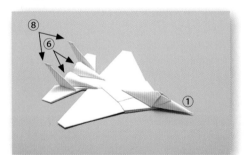

7 Component no. 1 is the nose and is glued on front of the airframe. Two components no. 6 are engines and are glued to the rear of the airframe. Two components no. 8 are vertical stabilizers and are glued vertically on both sides of the engines as shown in the figure.

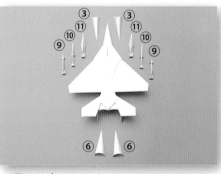

8 Then use components no. 3, 6, 9, 10, and 11 for the bottom half.

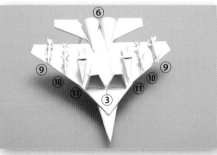

9 Two components no. 3 are air intakes and are glued on front of the airframe. Two components no. 6 are engines and are glued to the rear of the airframe. Components no. 9, 10, and 11 are missiles and are glued vertically on wings as shown in the figure.

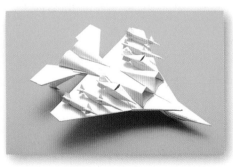

10 Reverse side.

11 Top view.

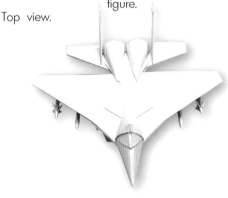

Rafale

Level of difficulty ★★★☆☆

Specifications

Contractor: Dassault
Crew: 1
Length: 50 ft, 3 in
Wingspan: 35 ft, 9 in
Height: 17 ft, 6 in
Max. Takeoff Weight: 47,400 lbs
Speed: 1,320 mph

Component No.	Method
❶	Basic component nine: Nose
❷	Special component: Canard, shown as follows
❸	Basic component two: Rhombus
❹	Special component: Wing, shown as follows
❺	Basic component six: Half cone
❻	Basic component one: Kite
❼	Basic component ten: Vertical stabilizer
❽	Basic component eleven
❾	Basic component fifteen: Missile no. 1
❿	Basic component sixteen: The combination of missile no. 2 and pylon
⓫	Basic component sixteen: The combination of missile no. 3 and pylon

All of the components needed for assembling a Rafale are shown in the figure below.

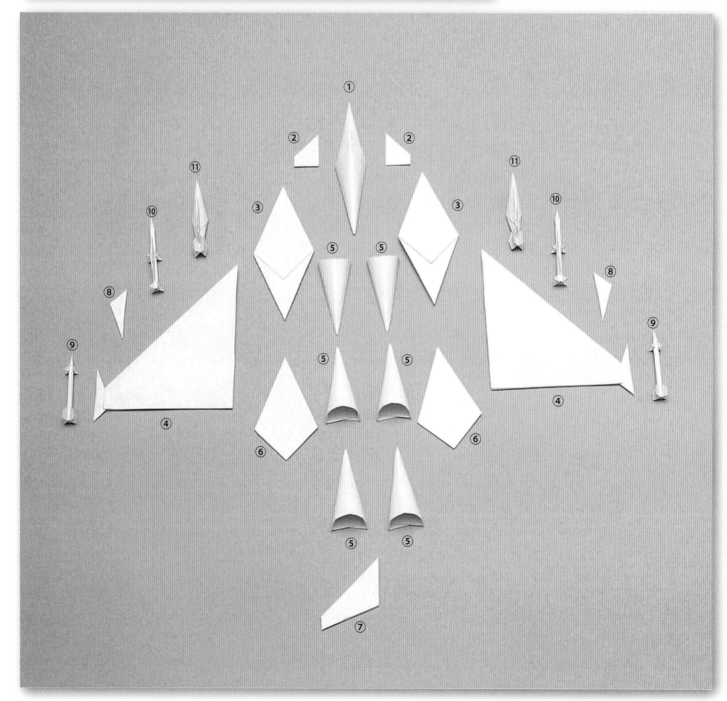

Methods for Special Components

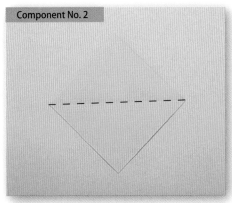

1 Use a square of size 1/16.

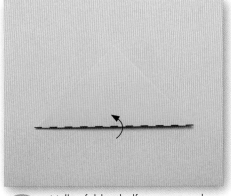

2 Valley fold in half into a triangle.

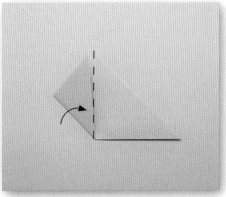

3 Valley fold the left corner to the center.

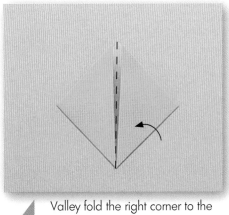

4 Valley fold the right corner to the center.

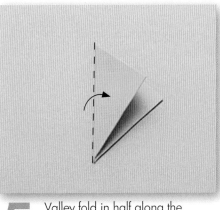

5 Valley fold in half along the center.

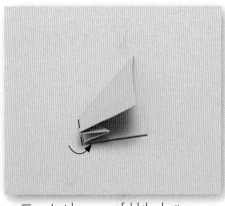

6 Inside reverse fold the bottom corner.

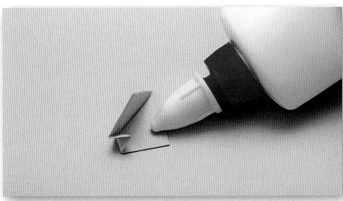

7 Use glue inside and cohere.

8 Done. Repeat to make two canards.

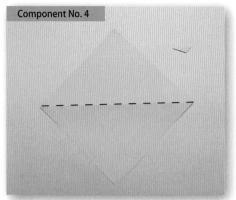

1 Start with a square of size 1 and a Basic component eleven.

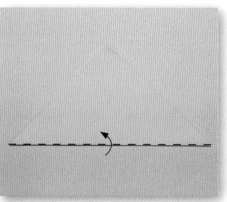

2 Use the square of size 1 and valley fold in half into a triangle.

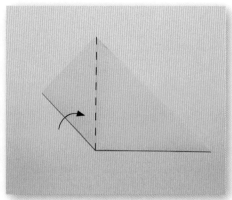

3 Valley fold the left corner to the center.

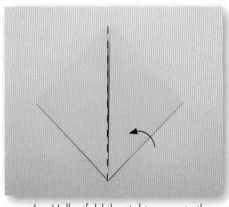

4 Valley fold the right corner to the center.

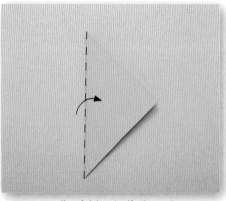

5 Valley fold in half along the center.

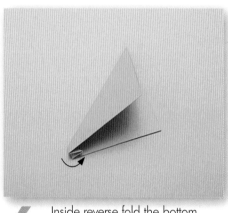

6 Inside reverse fold the bottom corner.

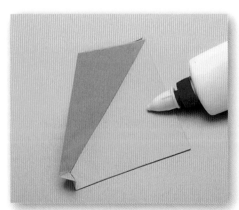

7 Use glue inside.

8 Glue the Basic component eleven inside as shown in the figure.

9 Done. Repeat to make two wings.

Assembly Procedure

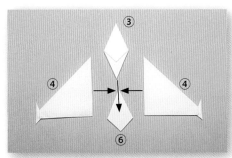

1 Use components no. 3, 4, and 6 for airframe.

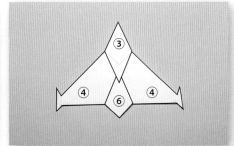

2 Glue component no. 6 to the bottom of component no. 3, and glue two components no. 4 on both sides for wings as shown in the figure.

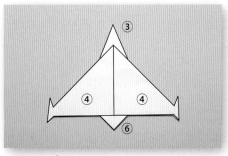

3 Flip over.

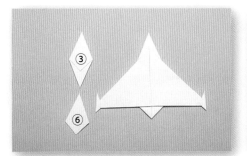

4 Then use the remaining components no. 3 and 6.

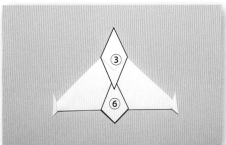

5 Glue components no. 3 and 6 to the airframe underbelly to match the top side.

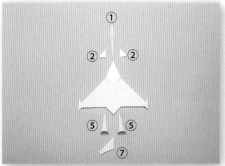

6 Use components no. 1, 2, 5, and 7 for the top half.

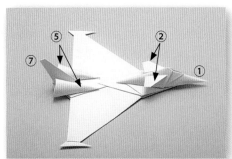

7 Component no. 1 is the nose and is glued on front of the airframe. Two components no. 2 are canards and are glued horizontally on both sides of the nose. Two components no. 5 are engines and are glued to the rear of the airframe. Component no. 7 is the vertical stabilizer and is glued vertically between engines as shown in the figure.

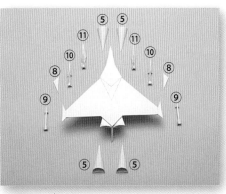

8 Then use components no. 5, 8, 9, 10, and 11 for the bottom half.

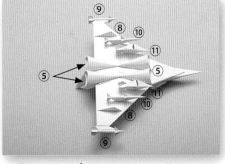

9 Two of components no. 5 are air intakes and are glued on front of the airframe. The other two components no. 5 are engines and are glued to the rear of the airframe. Two components no. 8 are glued vertically on wings. Two components no. 9 are missiles and are glued on both sides of wings. Components no. 10 and 11 are also missiles and are glued vertically on wings as shown in the figure.

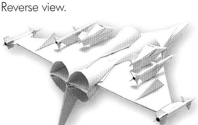

10 Reverse view.

11 Top view.

F-18
Hornet

Level of difficulty ★★★☆☆

Specifications

Contractor: McDonnell Douglas
Crew: 1
Length: 56 ft
Wingspan: 40 ft, 5 in
Height: 15 ft, 4 in
Empty Weight: 23,050 lbs
Max. Takeoff Weight: 51,900 lbs
Speed: Mach 1.7

Component No.	Method
1	Basic component nine: Nose
2	Basic component twelve
3	Basic component thirteen
4	Basic component three
5	Special component: Wing, shown as follows
6	Basic component one: Kite
7	Basic component six: Half cone
8	Basic component ten: Vertical stabilizer
9	Basic component ten: Vertical stabilizer
10	Basic component fifteen: Missile no. 1
11	Basic component sixteen: The combination of missile no. 2 and pylon
12	Basic component sixteen: The combination of missile no. 3 and pylon

All of the components needed for assembling an F/A-18 Hornet are shown in the figure below.

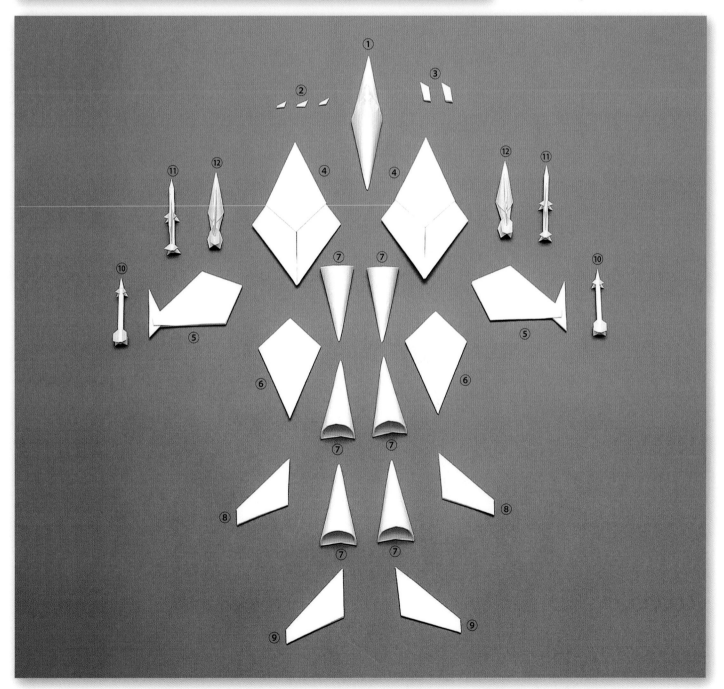

Methods for Special Components

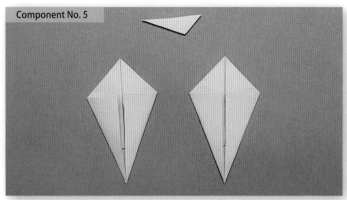

1 Start with two Kites and one Basic component eleven.

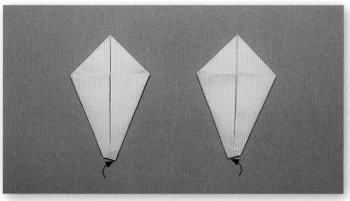

2 Take the two Kites and fold up the bottom corners.

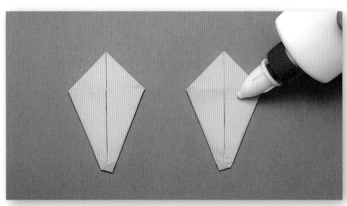

3 Use glue on one.

4 Glue the Basic component eleven between them as shown in the figure.

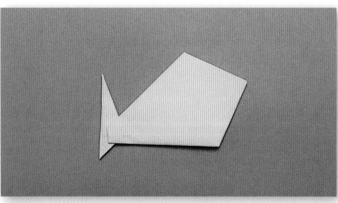

5 Done. Repeat to make two wings.

Assembly Procedure

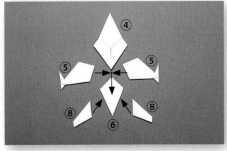

1 Use components no. 4, 5, 6, and 8 for airframe.

2 Glue component no. 6 to the bottom of component no. 4, glue two components no. 5 on both sides for wings, and glue two components no. 8 on both sides.

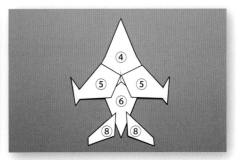

3 Flip over.

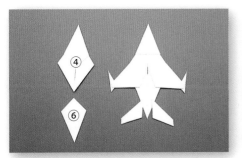

4 Then use the remaining components no. 4 and 6.

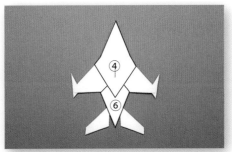

5 Glue components no. 4 and 6 to the airframe underbelly to match the top side.

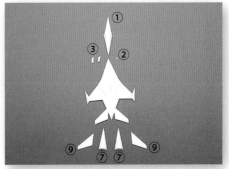

6 Use components no. 1, 2, 3, 7, and 9 for the top half.

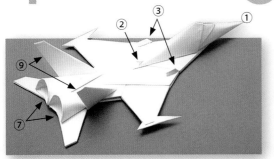

7 Component no. 1 is the nose and is glued on front of the airframe. Component no. 2 is glued in the rear of the nose vertically. Two components no. 3 are glued on both sides of the nose vertically. Two components no. 7 are engines and are glued to the rear of the airframe. Two components no. 9 are vertical stabilizers and are glued on both sides of the engines with an angle.

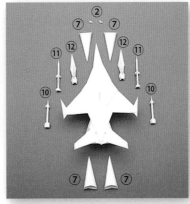

8 Then use components no. 2, 7, 10, 11, and 12 for the bottom half.

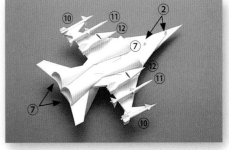

9 Two components no. 2 are glued on front of the airframe vertically. Two of components no. 7 are air intakes and are glued on front of the airframe. The other two components no. 7 are engines and are glued to the rear of the airframe. Two components no. 10 are missiles and are glued on both sides of wings. Components no. 11 and 12 are also missiles and are glued vertically on wings as shown in the figure.

10 Reverse side.

11 Top view.

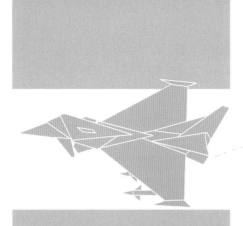

Typhoon

Specifications

Contractor: Eurofighter
Crew: 1
Length: 49 ft
Wingspan: 36 ft
Height: 17 ft
Empty Weight: 21,500 lbs
Max. Takeoff Weight: 46,300 lbs
Speed: 1,320 mph

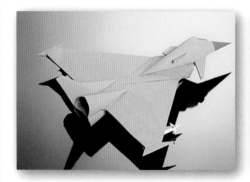
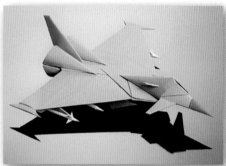

Component No.	Method
❶	Basic component nine: Nose
❷	Use squares of size $^1/_{16}$ to make Basic component ten: Vertical stabilizer
❸	Basic component thirteen
❹	Basic component two: Rhombus
❺	Basic component eight: Rectangular-based pyramid
❻	Special component: Wing, shown as follows
❼	Basic component one: Kite
❽	Basic component six: Half cone
❾	Basic component ten: Vertical stabilizer
❿	Basic component sixteen: The combination of missile no. 1 and pylon
⓫	Basic component sixteen: The combination of missile no. 2 and pylon
⓬	Basic component sixteen: The combination of missile no. 3 and pylon

All of the components needed for assembling a Typhoon are shown in the figure below.

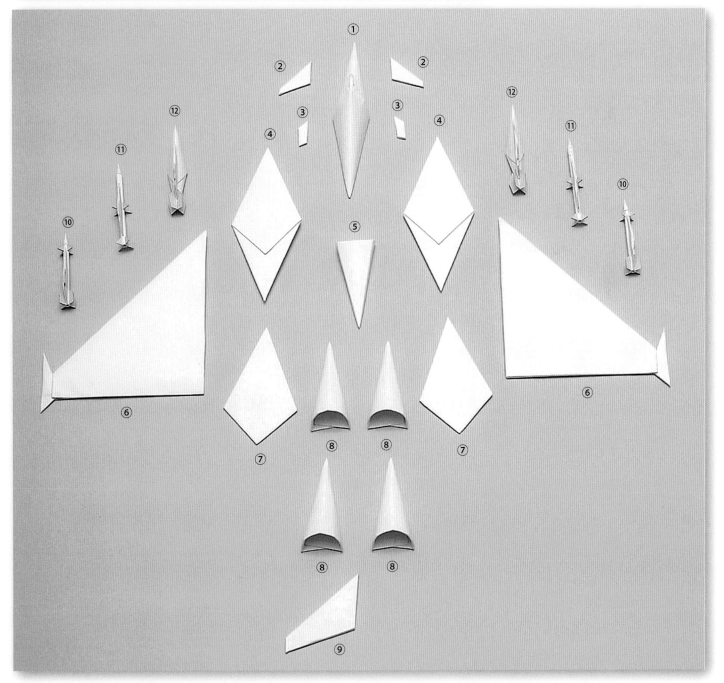

Methods for Special Components

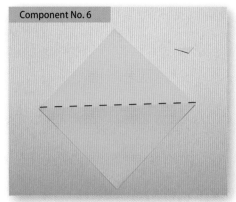

1 Start with a square of size 1 and a Basic component eleven.

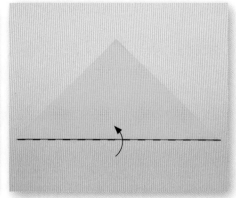

2 Take the square of size 1 and valley fold in half into a triangle.

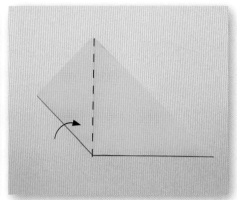

3 Valley fold the left corner to the center.

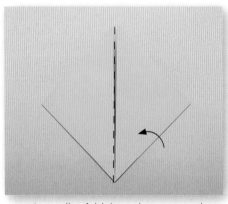

4 Valley fold the right corner to the center.

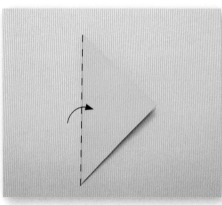

5 Valley fold in half along the center.

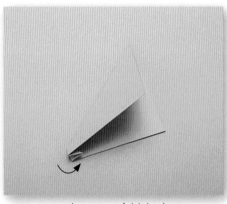

6 Inside reverse fold the bottom corner.

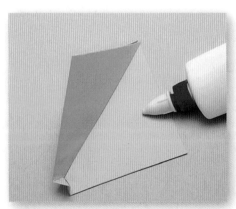

7 Use glue inside.

8 Glue the Basic component eleven inside as shown in the figure.

9 Done. Repeat to make two wings.

Component No. 6

Assembly Procedure

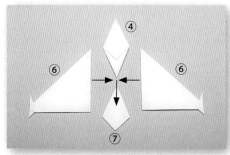

1 Use components no. 4, 6, and 7 for airframe.

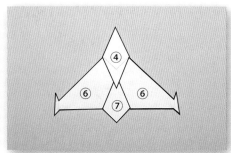

2 Glue component no. 7 to the bottom of component no. 4, and glue two components no. 6 on both sides for wings as shown in the figure.

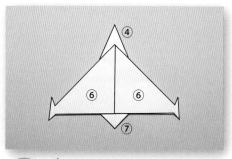

3 Flip over.

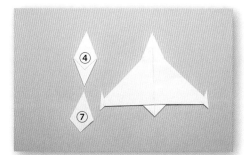

4 Then use the remaining components no. 4 and 7.

5 Glue components no. 4 and 7 to the airframe underbelly to match the top side.

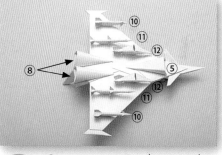

6 Use components no. 1, 2, 3, 8, and 9 for the top half.

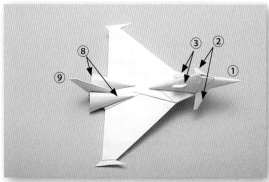

7 Component no. 1 is the nose and is glued on front of the airframe. Two components no. 2 are canards and are glued on both sides of the nose with an angle. Two components no. 3 are glued vertically on both sides of the nose. Two components no. 8 are engines and are glued to the rear of the airframe. Component no. 9 is the vertical stabilizer and is glued vertically between engines as shown in the figure.

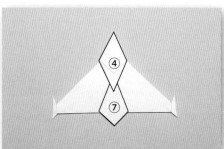

8 Then use components no. 5, 8, 10, 11, and 12 for the bottom half.

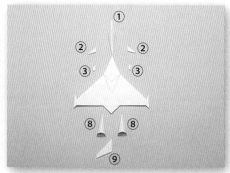

9 Component no. 5 is the air intake and is glued on front of the airframe. Two components no. 8 are engines and are glued to the rear of the airframe. Components no. 10, 11, and 12 are missiles and are glued vertically on wings as shown in the figure

10 Reverse side.

11 Top view.

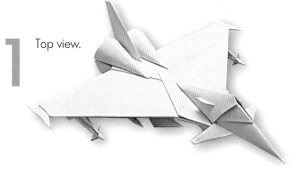

 Typhoon **81**

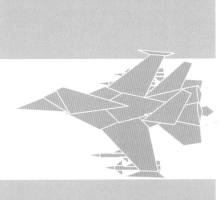

Su-27
Franker

Level of difficulty ★★★☆☆

Specifications

Contractor: Sukhoi
Crew: 1
Length: 71 ft, 12 in
Wingspan: 48 ft, 3 in
Height: 19 ft, 6 in
Empty Weight: 39,000 lbs
Max. Takeoff Weight: 66,140 lbs
Speed: 1,550 mph (Mach 2.3)

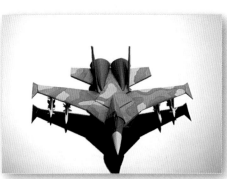

Component No.	Method
1	Basic component nine: Nose
2	Basic component three
3	Basic component seven: Trapezoid-based pyramid
4	Special component: Wing, shown as follows
5	Basic component one: Kite
6	Basic component six: Half cone
7	Special component, shown as follows
8	Basic component four: Horizontal stabilizer
9	Special component, shown as follows
10	Basic component ten: Vertical stabilizer
11	Basic component sixteen: The combination of missile no. 1 and pylon
12	Basic component sixteen: The combination of missile no. 2 and pylon

All of the components needed for assembling a Su-27 Franker are shown in the figure below.

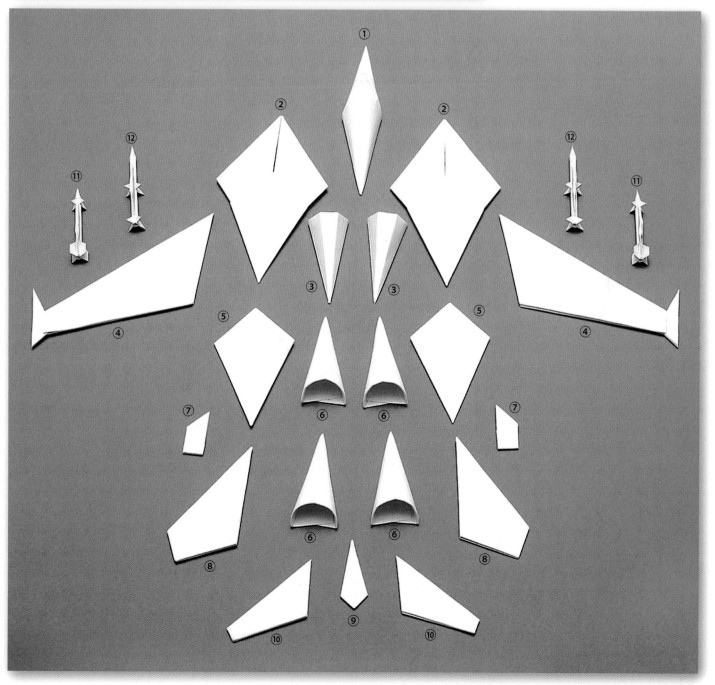

Methods for Special Components

Component No. 4

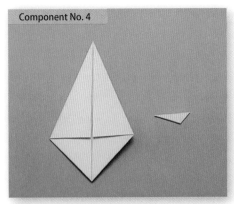

1 Use a Basic component eleven and use a square of size 1 to make a Kite.

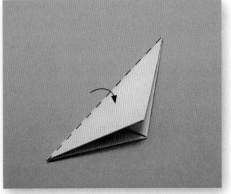

2 Take the Kite and valley fold in half along the center.

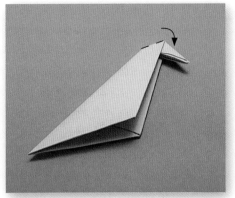

3 Inside reverse fold the top corner.

4 Cut along the edge to remove the protrusion.

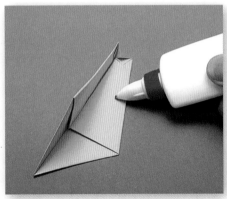

5 Use glue inside.

6 Glue the Basic component eleven inside as shown in the figure.

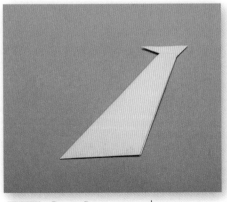

7 Done. Repeat to make two wings.

Component No. 7

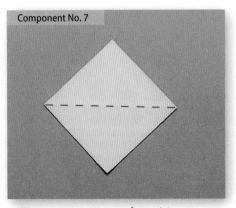

1 Use a square of size $1/16$.

2 Valley fold in half into a triangle.

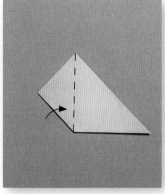

3 Valley fold the left corner to the center.

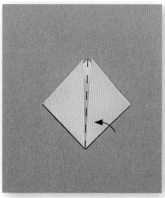

4 Valley fold the right corner to the center.

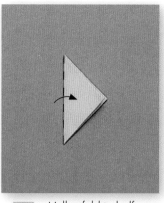

5 Valley fold in half along the center.

6 Inside reverse fold the bottom corner.

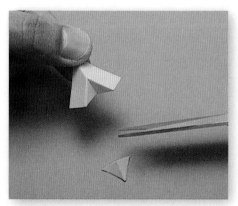

7 Cut off the protrusion.

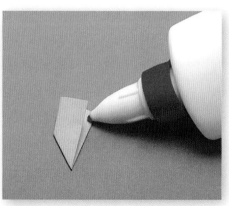

8 Use glue inside and cohere.

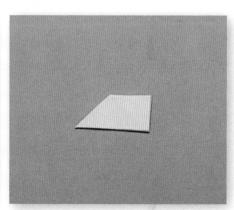

9 Done. Repeat to make two of these components.

Component No. 9

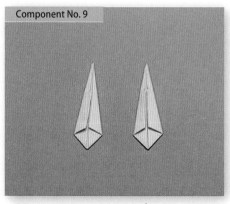

1 Use two squares of size $1/16$ to make two Basic components five.

2 Use glue on one part, and glue two parts to each other completely.

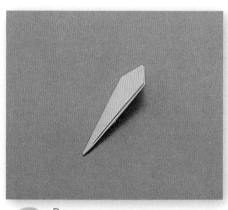

3 Done.

Assembly Procedure

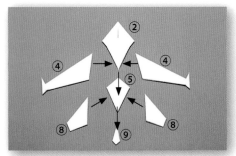

1 Use components no. 2, 4, 5, 8, and 9 for airframe.

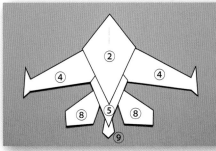

2 Glue component no. 5 to the bottom of component no. 2, and glue component no. 9 to the bottom of component no. 5, and glue two components no. 4 on both sides, and glue two components no. 8 on both sides.

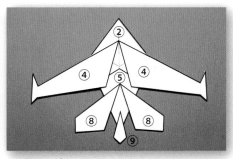

3 Flip over.

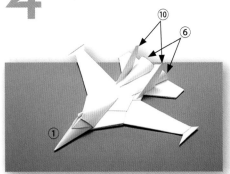

4 Then use the remaining components no. 2 and 5.

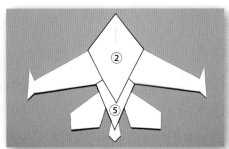

5 Glue components no. 2 and 5 to the airframe underbelly to match the top side.

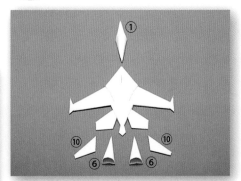

6 Use components no. 1, 6, and 10 for the top half.

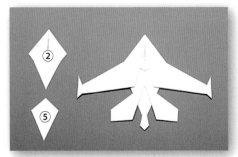

7 Component no. 1 is the nose and is glued on front of the airframe. Two components no. 6 are glued to the rear of the airframe. Two components no. 10 are vertical stabilizers and are glued vertically on both sides of the engines.

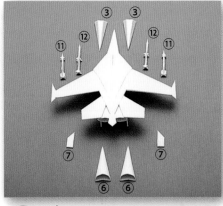

8 Then use components no. 3, 6, 7, 11, and 12 for the bottom half.

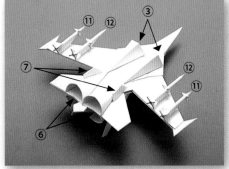

9 Two components no. 3 are air intakes and are glued on front of the airframe. Two components no. 6 are engines and are glued to the rear of the airframe. Two components no. 7 are glued vertically on both sides of engines, respectively. Components no. 11 and 12 are missiles and are glued vertically on wings as shown in the figure.

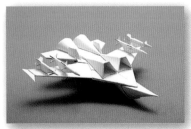

10 Reverse side.

11 Top view.

AC-130
Spector

Level of difficulty ★★★☆☆

Specifications

Contractor: Lockheed Martin
Crew: 14
Length: 97 ft, 9 in
Wingspan: 132 ft, 7 in
Height: 38 ft, 6 in
Empty Weight: 75,743 lbs
Max. Takeoff Weight: 175,000 lbs
Speed: 300 mph (Mach 0.4)

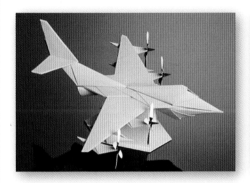

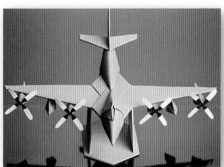

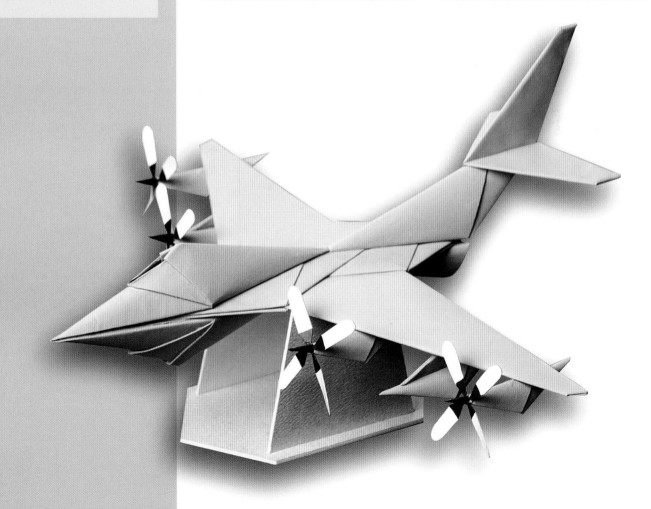

Component No.	Method
1	Basic component nine: Nose
2	Basic component two: Rhombus
3	Special component: Wing, shown as follows
4	Special component: Fuselage, shown as follows
5	Basic component six: Half cone
6	Special component: Fuselage, shown as follows
7	Basic component ten: Vertical stabilizer
8	Basic component ten: Vertical stabilizer
9	Special component: Fuel tank, shown as follows
10	Special component: Propeller, shown as follows

All of the components needed for assembling an AC-130 Specter are shown in the figure below.

Methods for Special Components

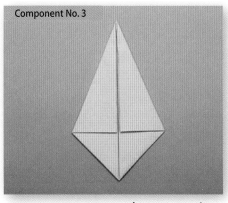

1 Use a square of size 1 to make a Kite.

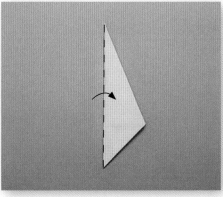

2 Valley fold in half along the center.

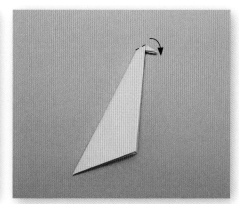

3 Inside reverse fold the top corner.

4 Cut along the edge to remove the protrusion.

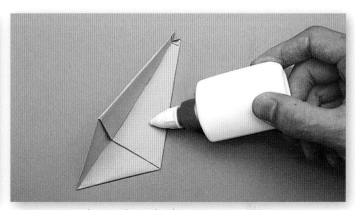

5 Use glue inside and cohere.

6 Done. Repeat to make two wings.

Component No. 4

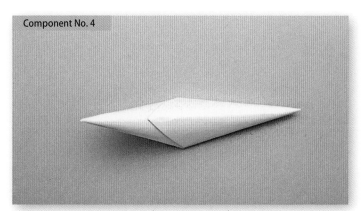

1 Use two squares of size ¹/4 to make a Basic component seventeen.

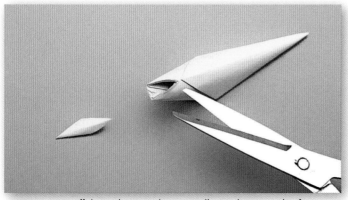

2 Cut off the tail corner horizontally as shown in the figure.

3 Done.

Component No. 6

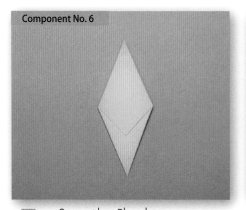

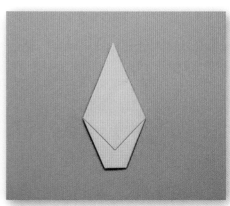

1 Start with a Rhombus.

2 Flip over and fold up the bottom corner.

3 Flip over and it's done. Repeat to make two Fuselages.

Component No. 9

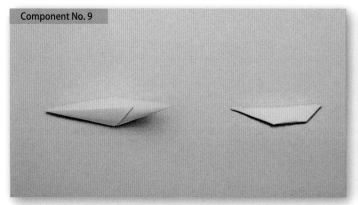

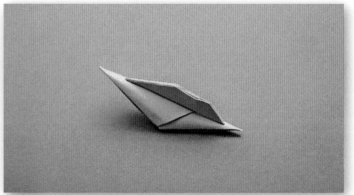

1 Start with a Pylon and a Basic component seventeen.

2 Use glue on the edge of the pylon and cohere to Basic component seventeen as shown in the figure and it's done. Repeat to make two fuel tanks.

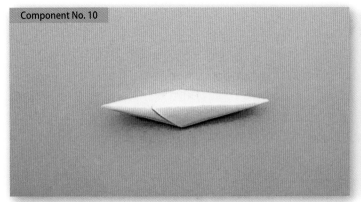

1 Start with a Basic component seventeen.

2 Cut two small chinks on the peak.

3 Similarly, cut two small chinks on the peak in the back side.

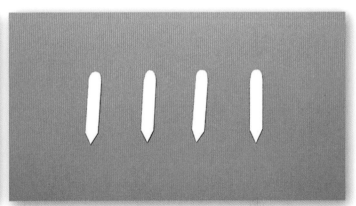

4 Then cut four propellers using cardboard as shown in the figure.

5 Use glue on the tip of four propellers and cohere into the four chinks on the peak as shown in the figure and it's done. Repeat three times to make four propellers total.

AC-130 Spector   **9 1**

Assembly Procedure

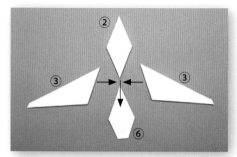

1 Use components no. 2, 3, and 6 for the airframe.

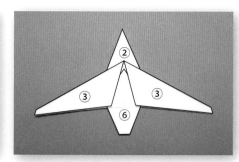

2 Glue component no. 6 to the bottom of component no. 2, and glue two components no. 3 on both sides for wings as shown in the figure.

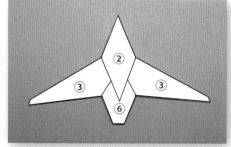

3 Flip over.

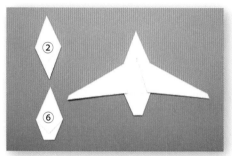

4 Then use the remaining components no. 2 and 6.

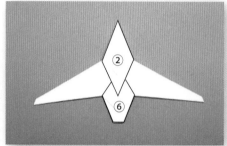

5 Glue components no. 2 and 6 to the airframe underbelly to match the top side.

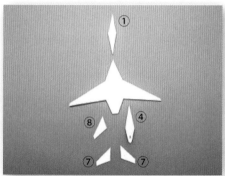

6 Use components no. 1, 4, 7, and 8 for the top half.

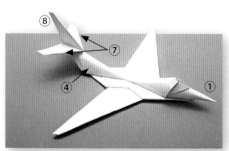

7 Component no. 1 is the nose and is glued on the front of the airframe. Component no. 4 is glued to the rear of the airframe. Component no. 8 is the vertical stabilizer and is glued vertically on the top of component no. 4. Two components no. 7 make up the horizontal stabilizer and are glued horizontally on both sides of the vertical stabilizer as shown in the figure.

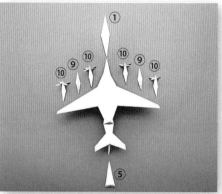

8 Then use components no. 1, 5, 9, and 10 for the bottom half.

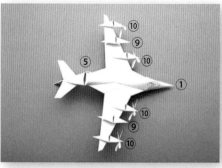

9 Component no. 1 is the nose in the front of the airframe; glue to the nose section on the top half. Component no. 5 is glued to the rear of the airframe. Two components no. 9 are fuel tanks and are glued on wings. Four components no. 10 are propellers and are glued on wings as shown in the figure.

10 Reverse side.

11 Top view.

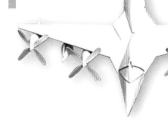

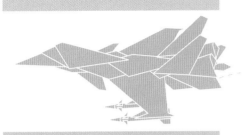

Su-35

Specifications

Contractor: Sukhoi
Crew: 1
Length: 72 feet, 10 in
Wingspan: 49 feet, 8 in
Height: 20 feet, 10 in
Empty Weight: 37,500 lbs
Max. Takeoff Weight: 75,000 lbs
Speed: 1,550 mph (Mach 2.3)
Range: 4,000 miles

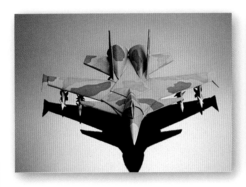

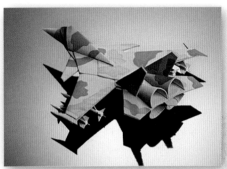

Component No.	Method
❶	Basic component nine: Nose
❷	Basic component one: Kite
❸	Basic component ten: Vertical stabilizer
❹	Basic component seven: Trapezoid-based pyramid
❺	Basic component three
❻	Special component: Wing, shown as follows
❼	Basic component six: Half cone
❽	Basic component one: Kite
❾	Special component, shown as follows
❿	Basic component four: Horizontal stabilizer
⓫	Special component, shown as follows
⓬	Basic component ten: Vertical stabilizer
⓭	Basic component sixteen: The combination of missile no. 1 and pylon
⓮	Basic component sixteen: The combination of missile no. 2 and pylon

All of the components needed for assembling a Su-35 Flanker are shown in the figure below.

Methods for Special Components

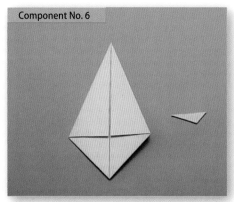

1 Use a Basic component eleven and use a square of size 1 to make a Kite.

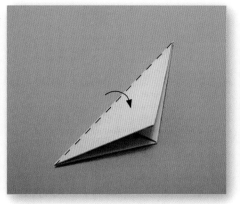

2 Take the Kite and valley fold in half along the center.

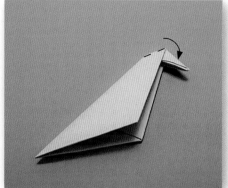

3 Inside reverse fold the top corner.

4 Cut along the edge to remove the protrusion.

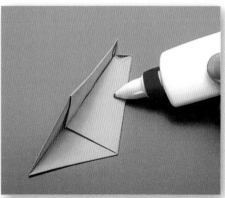

5 Use glue inside.

6 Glue the Basic component eleven inside as shown in the figure.

7 Done. Repeat to make two wings.

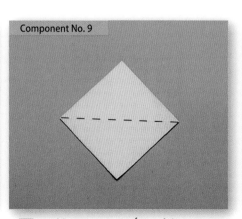

1 Use a square of size 1/16.

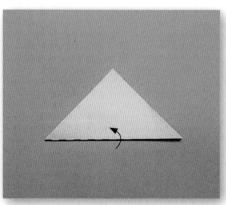

2 Valley fold in half into a triangle.

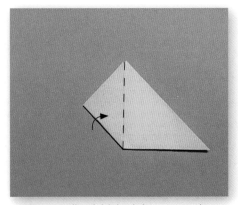

3 Valley fold the left corner to the center.

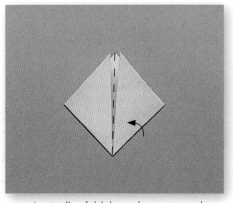

4 Valley fold the right corner to the center.

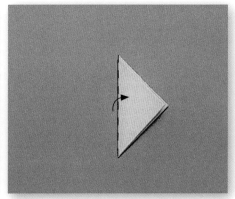

5 Valley fold in half along the center.

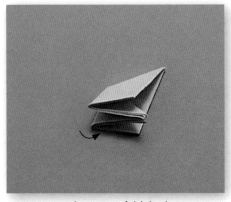

6 Inside reverse fold the bottom corner.

7 Cut off the protrusion.

8 Use glue inside and cohere.

9 Done. Repeat to make two of these components.

Component No. 11

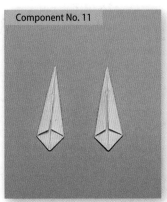

1 Use two squares of size $1/16$ to make two Basic components five.

2 Use glue on one part, and glue two parts to each other completely.

3 Done.

Assembly Procedure

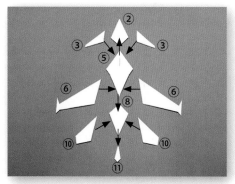

1 Use components no. 2, 3, 5, 6, 8, 10, and 11 for airframe.

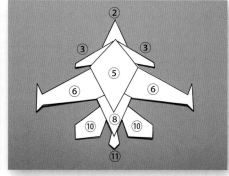

2 Glue component no. 5 to the bottom of component no. 2, and glue component no. 8 to the bottom of component no. 5, and glue component no. 11 to the bottom of component no. 8, and from top to bottom on both sides, glue two components no. 3; glue two components no. 6 for wings; glue two components no. 10 for horizontal stabilizers.

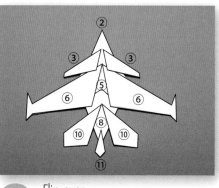

3 Flip over.

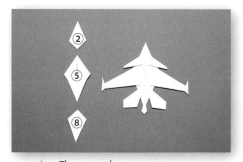

4 Then use the remaining components no. 2, 5, and 8.

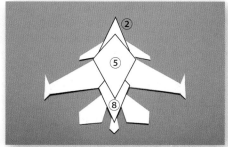

5 Glue components no. 2, 5, and 8 to the airframe underbelly to match the top side.

6 Use components no. 1, 7, and 12 for the top half.

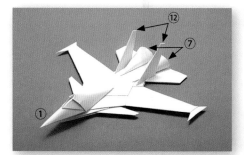

7 Component no. 1 is the nose and is glued on front of the airframe. Two components no. 7 are engines and are glued to the rear of the airframe. Two components no. 12 are vertical stabilizers and are glued vertically on both sides of engines as shown in the figure.

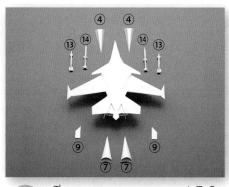

8 Then use components no. 4, 7, 9, 13, and 14 for the bottom half.

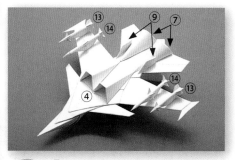

9 Two components no. 4 are air intakes and are glued on front of the airframe. Two components no. 7 are engines and are glued to the rear of the airframe. Two components no. 9 are glued vertically on both sides of engines, respectively. Components no. 13 and 14 are missiles and are glued vertically on wings as shown in the figure.

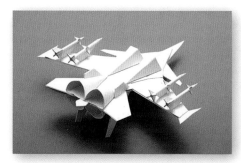

10 Reverse side.

11 Top view.

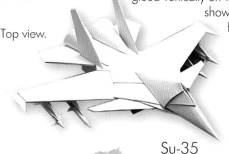

Su-35

JAS39
Gripen

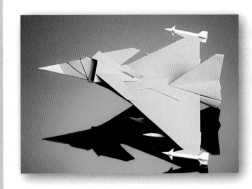

Level of difficulty ★★★★☆

Specifications

Contractor: Saab
Crew: 1
Length: 46 ft, 3 in
Wingspan: 27 ft, 7 in
Height: 14 ft, 9 in
Empty Weight: 14,600 lbs
Max. Takeoff Weight: 27,560 lbs
Speed: 1,320 mph

Component No.	Method
❶	Basic component nine: Nose
❷	Basic component thirteen
❸	Basic component twelve
❹	Special component: Canard, shown as follows
❺	Basic component eight: Rectangular-based pyramid
❻	Basic component two: Rhombus
❼	Special component: Fuel tank, shown as follows
❽	Special component: Wing, shown as follows
❾	Basic component one: Kite
❿	Basic component six: Half cone
⓫	Special component: Vertical stabilizer, shown as follows
⓬	Basic component fifteen: Missile no. 1
⓭	Basic component sixteen: The combination of missile no. 2 and pylon
⓮	Basic component sixteen: The combination of missile no. 3 and pylon

All of the components needed for assembling a JAS39 Gripen are shown in the figure below.

Methods for Special Components

Component No. 4

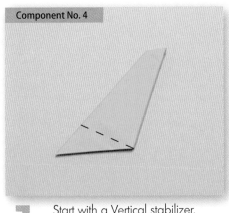

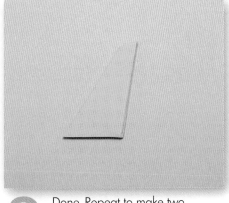

1 Start with a Vertical stabilizer. Then cut along the dahsed line shown in the figure.

2 After cutting, keep only the top section.

3 Done. Repeat to make two canards.

Component No. 7

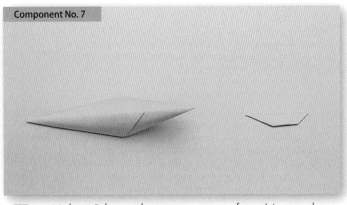

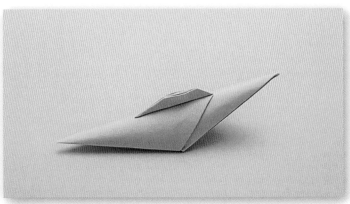

1 Make a Pylon and use two squares of size $1/4$ to make a Basic component seventeen.

2 Use glue on the edge of the Pylon and glue to Basic component seventeen vertically. Done.

Component No. 7

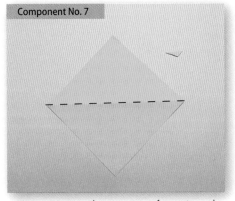

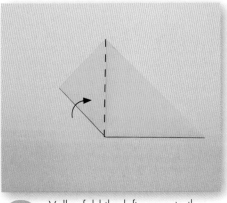

1 Start with a square of size 1 and a Basic component eleven.

2 Use the square of size 1, and valley fold in half into a triangle.

3 Valley fold the left corner to the center.

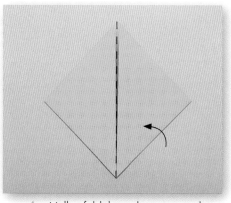

4 Valley fold the right corner to the center.

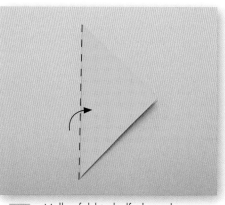

5 Valley fold in half along the center.

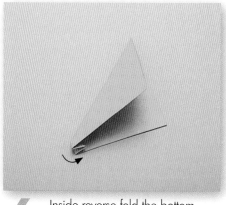

6 Inside reverse fold the bottom corner.

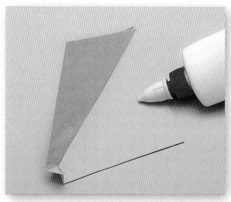

7 Use glue inside.

8 Glue the Basic component eleven inside as shown in the figure.

9 Done. Repeat to make two wings.

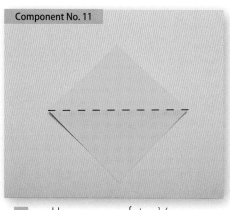

Component No. 11

1 Use a square of size 1/4.

2 Valley fold in half into a triangle.

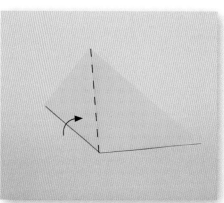

3 Valley fold the left corner to the center.

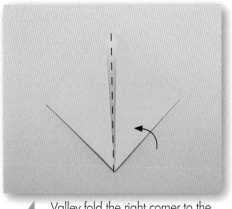

4 Valley fold the right corner to the center.

5 Valley fold in half along the center.

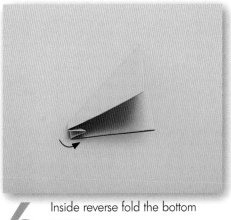

6 Inside reverse fold the bottom corner.

7 Use glue inside and cohere.

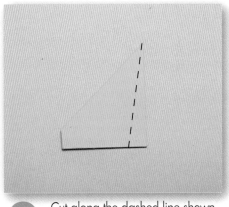

8 Cut along the dashed line shown in the figure.

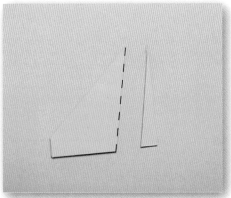

9 After cutting, keep only the left section.

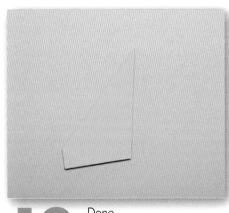

10 Done.

Assembly Procedure

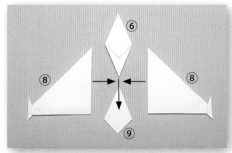

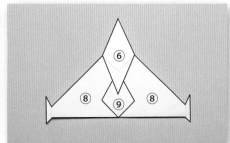

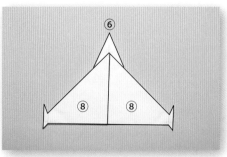

1 Use components no. 6, 8, and 9 for airframe.

2 Glue component no. 9 to the bottom of component no. 6, and glue two components no. 8 on both sides for wings.

3 Flip over.

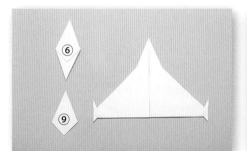

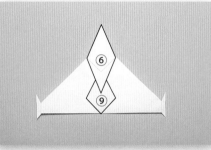

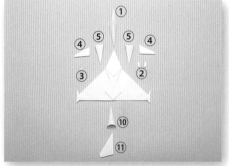

4 Then use the remaining components no. 6 and 9.

5 Glue components no. 6 and 9 to the airframe underbelly to match the top side.

6 Use components no. 1, 2, 3, 4, 5, 10, and 11 for the top half.

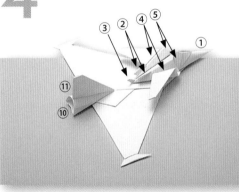

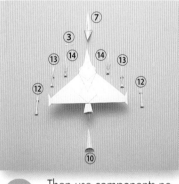

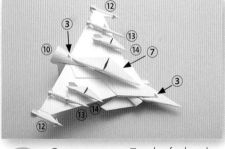

7 Component no. 1 is the nose and is glued on front of the airframe. Two components no. 5 are air intakes and are glued on both sides of the nose. Two components no. 4 are canards and are glued horizontally on both sides of air intakes. Two components no. 2 are glued vertically on two air intakes. Component no. 3 is glued vertically on the airframe. Component no. 10 is glued to the rear of the airframe. Component no. 11 is the vertical stabilizer and is glued vertically on the engine.

8 Then use components no. 3, 7, 10, 12, 13, and 14 for the bottom half.

9 Component no. 7 is the fuel tank and is glued to the center of the airframe. Component no. 10 is the engine and is glued to the rear of the airframe. One of component no. 3 is glued on front of the airframe, and another is glued on the engine, both vertically. Two components no. 12 are missiles and are glued on both sides of wings. Components no. 13 and 14 are also missiles and are glued on wings as shown in the figure.

11 Top view.

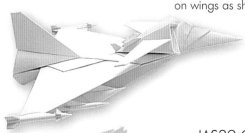

10 Reverse side.

AJ37
Viggen

Level of difficulty ★★★★☆

Specifications

Contractor: Saab
Crew: 1
Length: 53 ft, 9 in
Wingspan: 34 ft, 9 in
Height: 19 ft, 4 in
Max. Takeoff Weight: 45,194 lbs
Speed: 1,320 mph (Mach 2.0)

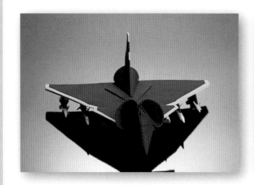

Component No.	Method
❶	Basic component nine: Nose
❷	Basic component six: Half cone
❸	Special component: Canard, shown as follows
❹	Basic component five
❺	Special component: Fuel tank, shown as follows
❻	Special component: Wing, shown as follows
❼	Basic component one: Kite
❽	Basic component six: Half cone
❾	Special component: Vertical stabilizer, shown as follows
❿	Basic component sixteen: The combination of missile no. 1 and pylon
⓫	Basic component sixteen: The combination of missile no. 2 and pylon
⓬	Basic component sixteen: The combination of missile no. 3 and pylon

All of the components needed for assembling an AJ37 Viggen are shown in the figure below.

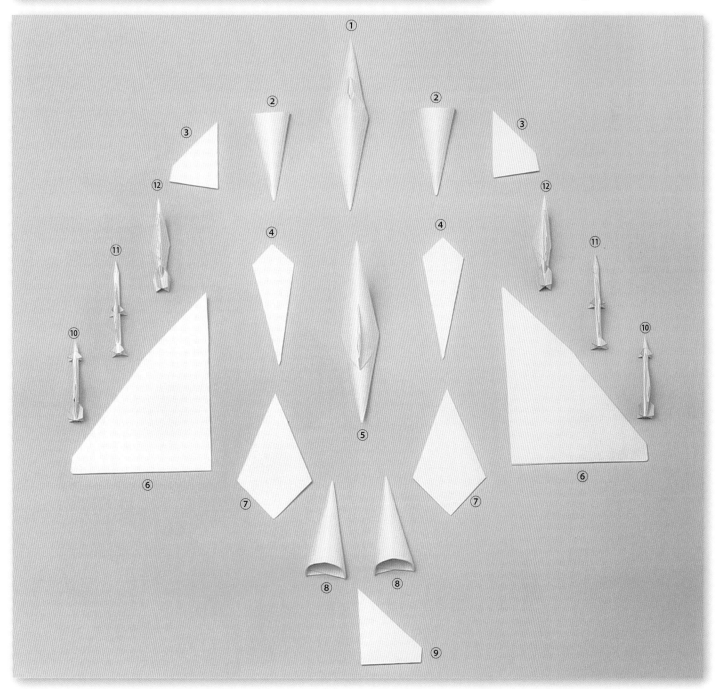

Methods for Special Components

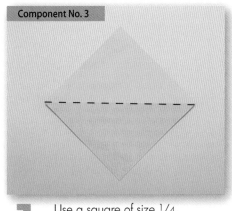

1 Use a square of size ¹/4.

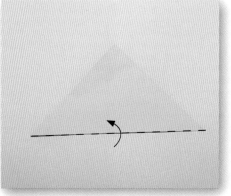

2 Valley fold in half into a triangle.

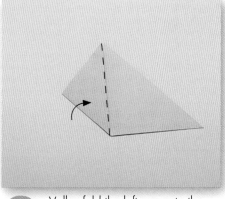

3 Valley fold the left corner to the center.

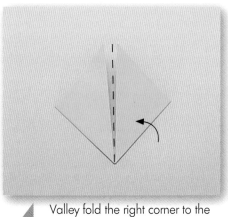

4 Valley fold the right corner to the center.

5 Valley fold in half along the center.

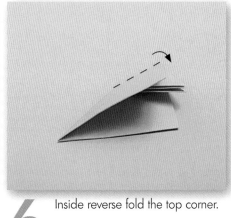

6 Inside reverse fold the top corner.

7 Cut along the edge to remove the protrusion.

8 Use glue inside and cohere.

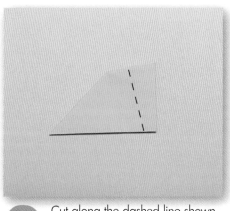

9 Cut along the dashed line shown in the figure.

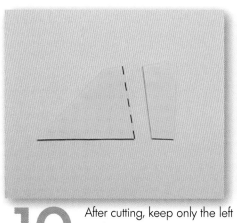

10 After cutting, keep only the left section.

11 Done. Repeat to make two canards.

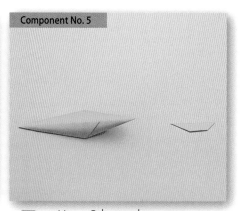

1 Use a Pylon and two squares of size $1/4$ to make a Basic component seventeen.

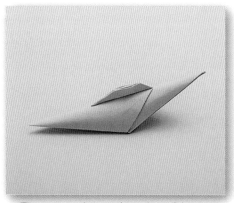

2 Use glue on the edge of the Pylon and cohere to Basic component seventeen as shown in figure and it's done.

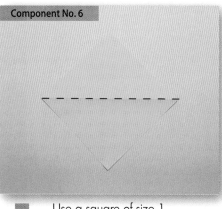

1 Use a square of size 1.

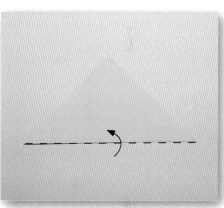

2 Valley fold in half into a triangle

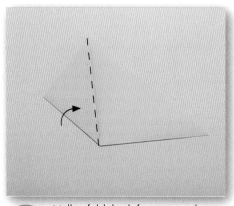

3 Valley fold the left corner to the center.

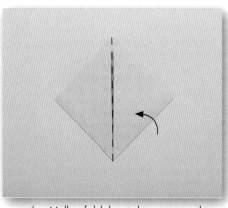

4 Valley fold the right corner to the center.

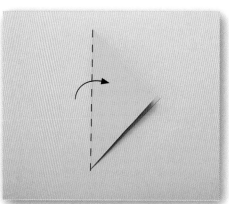

5 Valley fold in half along the center.

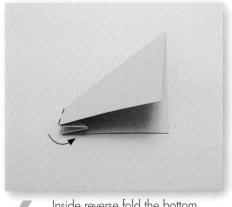

6 Inside reverse fold the bottom corner.

7 Cut along the dashed line shown in the figure.

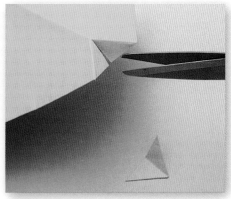

8 And cut along the central crease.

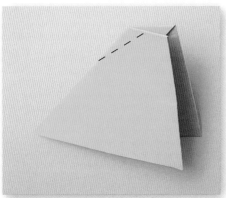

9 After cutting, inside reverse fold along the dashed line shown in the figure.

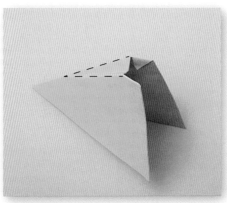

10 Inside reverse fold as shown in the figure.

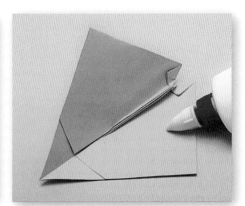

11 Use glue inside.

12 Use glue on the insde reverse fold part and cohere.

13 Done. Repeat to make two wings.

Component No. 9

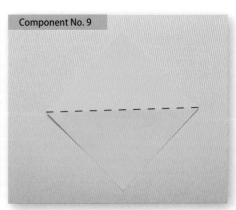

1 Use a square of size ¹/4.

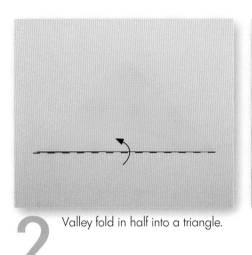

2 Valley fold in half into a triangle.

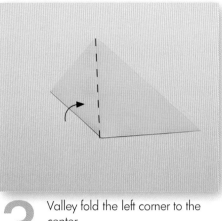

3 Valley fold the left corner to the center.

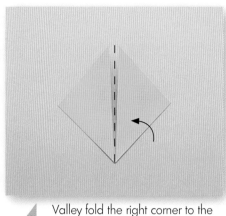

4 Valley fold the right corner to the center.

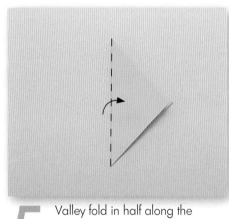

5 Valley fold in half along the center.

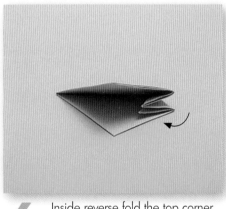

6 Inside reverse fold the top corner.

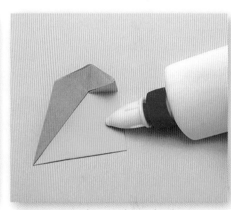

7 Use glue inside and cohere.

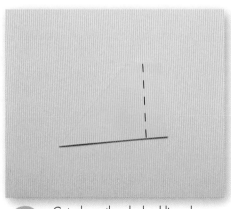

8 Cut along the dashed line shown in the figure.

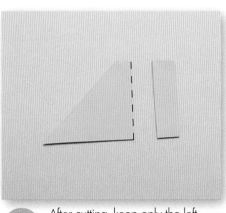

9 After cutting, keep only the left section.

10 Done.

Assembly Procedure

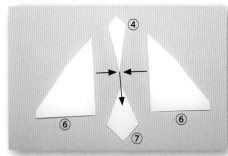

1 Use components no. 4, 6, and 7 for airframe.

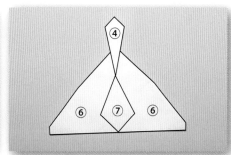

2 Glue component no. 7 to the bottom of component no. 4, and glue two components no. 6 on both sides for wings.

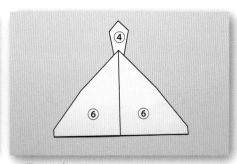

3 Flip over.

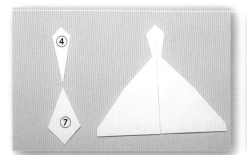

4 Then use the remaining components no. 4 and 7.

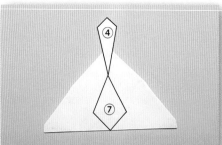

5 Glue components no. 4 and 7 to the airframe underbelly to match the top side.

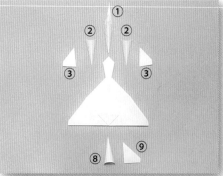

6 Use components no. 1, 2, 3, 8, and 9 for the top half.

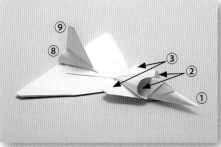

7 Component no. 1 is the nose and is glued on front of the airframe. Two components no. 2 are air intakes and are glued on both sides of the nose. Two components no. 3 are canards and are glued horizontally on both sides of the air intakes. Component no. 8 is the engine and is glued to the rear of the airframe. Component no. 9 is glued vertically on the engine.

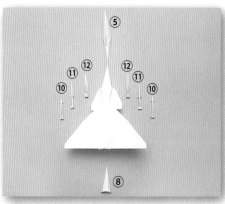

8 Then use components no. 5, 8, 10, 11, and 12 for the bottom half.

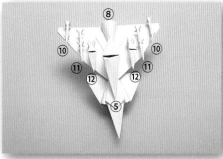

9 Component no. 5 is the fuel tank and is glued to the center of the airframe. Component no. 8 is the engine and is glued to the rear of the airframe. Components no. 10, 11, and 12 are missiles and are glued vertically on wings as shown in the figure.

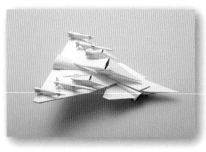

10 Reverse side.

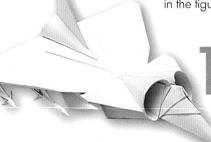

11 Top view.

Mirage
2000

Level of difficulty ★★★★☆

Specifications

Contractor: Dassault
Crew: 1
Length: 50 ft, 3 in
Wingspan: 29 ft, 5 in
Height: 17 ft
Empty Weight: 16,750 lbs
Max. Takeoff Weight: 37,480 lbs
Speed: 1,450 mph
Range: 900 miles

Component No.	Method
1	Basic component nine: Nose
2	Special component: Air intake, shown as follows
3	Basic component thirteen
4	Basic component two: Rhombus
5	Special component: Fuel tank, shown as follows
6	Special component: Wing, shown as follows
7	Special component: Fuselage, shown as follows
8	Basic component six: Half cone
9	Special component: Fuselage, shown as follows
10	Basic component ten: Vertical stabilizer
11	Basic component sixteen: The combination of missile no. 1 and pylon
12	Basic component sixteen: The combination of missile no. 2 and pylon

All of the components needed for assembling a Mirage 2000 are shown in the figure below.

Methods for Special Components

Component No. 2

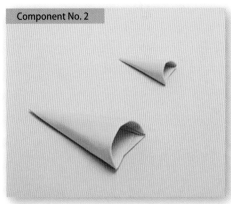

1 Use a square of size $1/4$ and a square of size $1/16$ to make two Half cones.

2 Place them face to face.

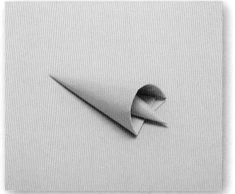

3 Use glue on the bottom of the small Half cone and glue it into the big Half cone asnd it's done. Repeat to make two air intakes.

Component No. 5

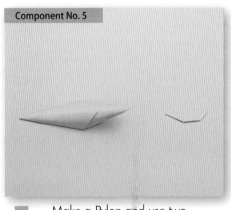

1 Make a Pylon and use two squares of size $1/4$ to make a Basic component seventeen.

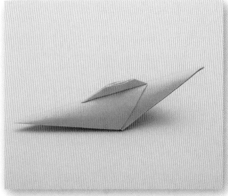

2 Use glue on the edge of the Pylon and cohere to the Basic component seventeen, as shown in figure, and it's done.

Component No. 6

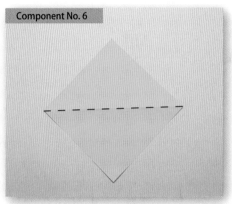

1 Use a square of size 1.

2 Valley fold in half into a triangle.

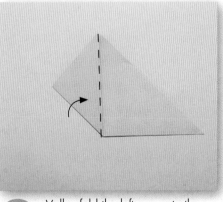

3 Valley fold the left corner to the center.

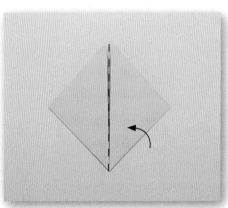

4 Valley fold the right corner to the center.

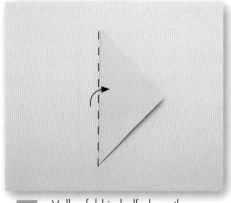

5 Valley fold in half along the center.

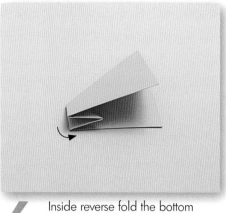

6 Inside reverse fold the bottom corner.

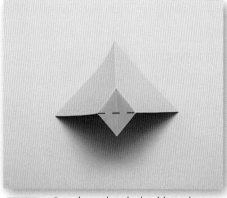

7 Cut along the dashed line shown in the figure.

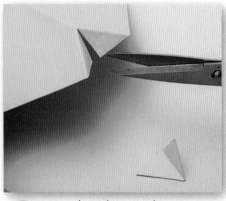

8 Cut along the central crease.

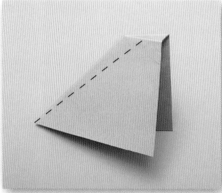

9 After cutting, inside reverse fold along the dashed line shown in the figure.

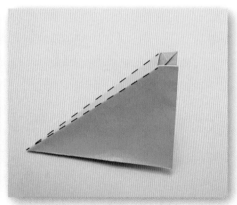

10 Inside reverse fold as shown in the figure.

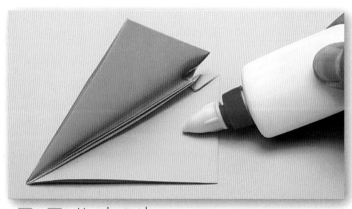

11 Use glue inside.

12 And use glue on the inside reverse fold part and cohere.

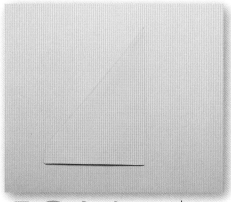

13 Done. Repeat to make two wings.

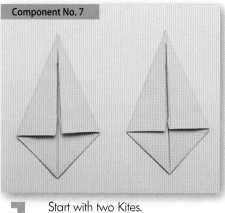

1 Start with two Kites.

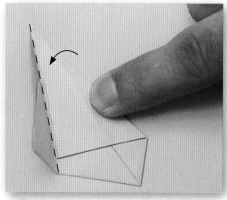

2 Take one and open it. Valley fold the right edge to the left crease.

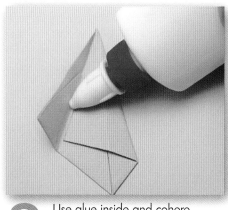

3 Use glue inside and cohere.

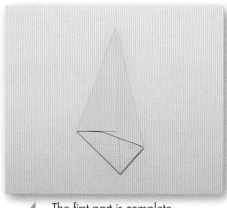

4 The first part is complete.

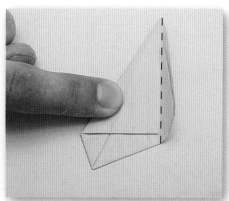

5 Similarly, take the other and open it. Valley fold the left edge to the right crease.

6 Use glue inside and cohere.

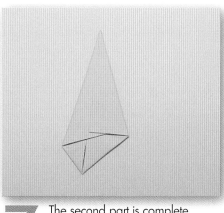

7 The second part is complete.

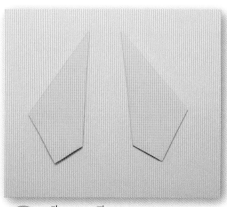

8 Flip over. These two parts are a pair of fuselage. Repeat to make two pairs.

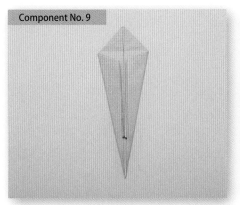

1 Start with a Basic component five.

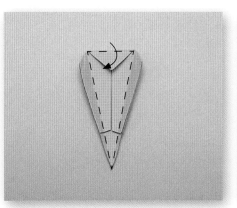

2 Open it and fold down the top corner to the creases.

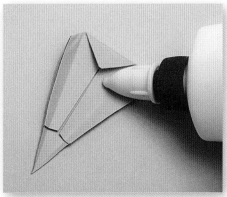

3 Use glue inside and cohere.

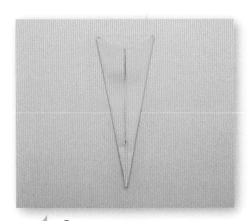

4 Done.

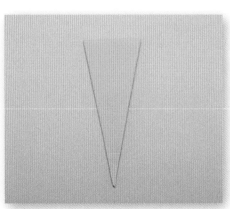

5 Flip over. Repeat to make two fuselages.

Assembly Procedure

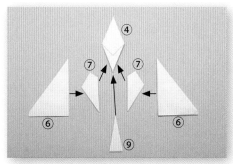

1 Use components no. 4, 6, 7, and 9 for airframe.

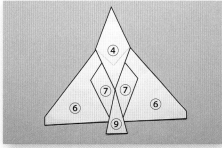

2 Glue two components no. 7 to the bottom of component no. 4, glue component no. 9 on them, and glue two components no. 6 on both sides for wings, as shown in the figure.

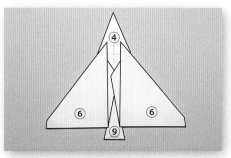

3 Flip over.

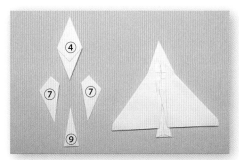

4 Then use the remaining components no. 4, 7, and 9.

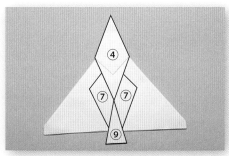

5 Glue components no. 4, 7, and 9 to the airframe underbelly to match the top side.

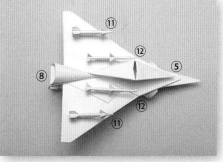

6 Use components no. 1, 2, 3, 8, and 10 for the top half.

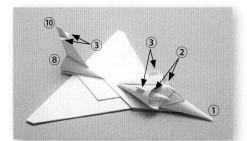

7 Component no. 1 is glued on front of the airframe. Two components no. 2 are air intakes and are glued on both sides of the nose. Component no. 8 is the engine and is glued to the rear of the airframe. Component no. 10 is the vertical stabilizer and is glued vertically on the engine. Two of components no. 3 are glued vertically on air intakes. The other two components no. 3 are glued horizontally on both sides of the vertical stabilizer.

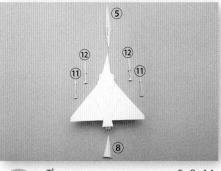

8 Then use components no. 5, 8, 11, and 12 for the bottom half.

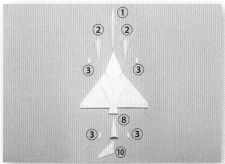

9 Component no. 5 is the fuel tank and is glued to the center of the airframe. Component no. 8 is the engine and is glued to the rear of the airframe. Components no. 11, and 12 are missiles and are glued on wings as shown in the figure.

10 Reverse side.

11 Top view.

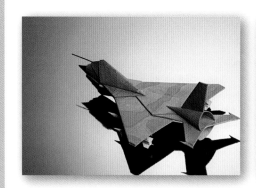

MiG-21
Fishbed

Level of difficulty ★★★★☆

Specifications

Contractor: Mikoyan-Gurevich
Crew: 1
Length: 51 ft, 8 in
Wingspan: 23 ft, 5 in
Height: 13 ft, 5 in
Empty Weight: 12,880 lbs
Max. Takeoff Weight: 21,600 lbs
Speed: 1,350 mph (Mach 2)
Range: 600 miles

Component No.	Method
1	Special component, shown as follows
2	Use squares of size $^1/_{16}$ to make Basic component six: Half cone
3	Special component: Nose, shown as follows
4	Basic component one: Kite
5	Special component: Wing, shown as follows
6	Basic component six: Half cone
7	Basic component two: Rhombus
8	Basic component ten: Vertical stabilizer
9	Basic component eleven
10	Special component: Horizontal stabilizer, shown as follows
11	Basic component sixteen: The combination of missile no. 1 and pylon
12	Basic component sixteen: The combination of missile no. 2 and pylon

All of the components needed for assembling a MiG-21 Fishbed are shown in the figure below.

Methods for Special Components

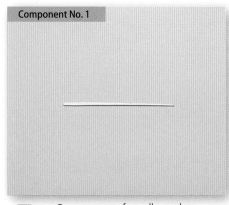

1 Cut a piece of cardboard as shown in the figure.

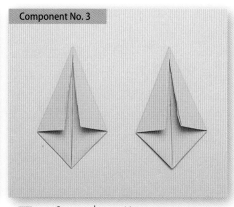

1 Start with two Kites.

2 Take one of them and flip over. Fold up the bottom corner.

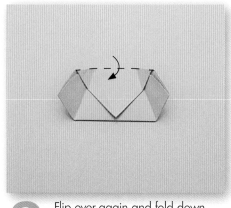

3 Flip over again and fold down the top corner.

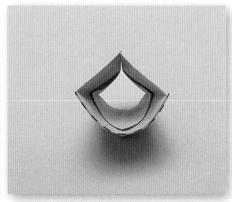

4 Curl the edge to a curve along the dashed line shown in the figure.

5 Use glue on one side.

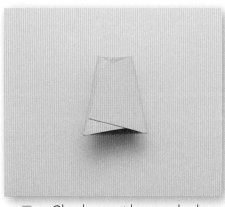

6 Glue the two sides to each other.

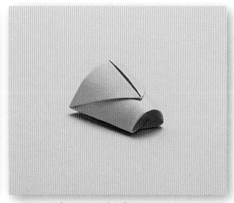

7 Flip over. The first part is complete.

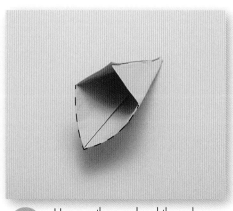

8 Use another and curl the edge to a curve along the dashed line shown in the figure.

9 Use glue on one side.

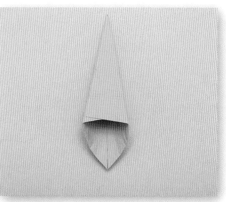

10 Glue the two sides to each other.

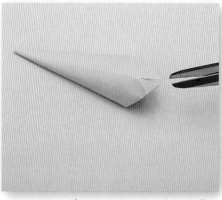

11 Flip over again. Cut a small gap along the center.

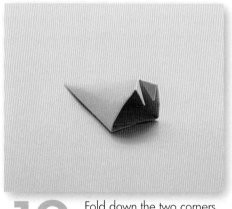

12 Fold down the two corners from the small gap.

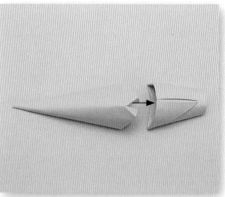

13 Place the two parts face to face.

14 Tuck the two corners on the second part into the chink on the first part, and use glue inside to fix tightly. You can use some sharp tools if it is difficult to tuck in.

15 Done. Repeat to make two noses.

Component No. 5

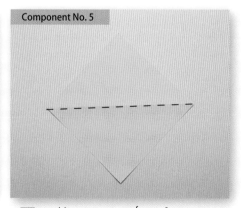

1 Use a square of size 1.

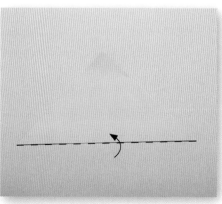

2 Valley fold in half into a triangle.

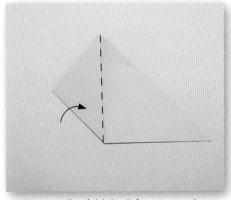

3 Valley fold the left corner to the center.

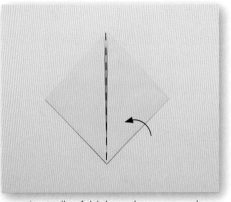

4 Valley fold the right corner to the center.

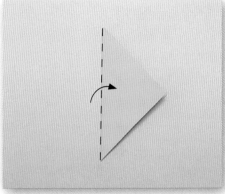

5 Valley fold in half along the center.

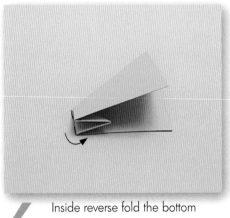

6 Inside reverse fold the bottom corner.

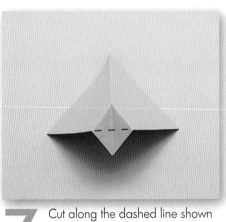

7 Cut along the dashed line shown in the figure.

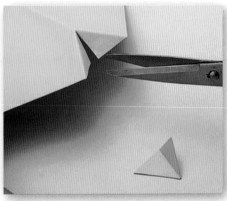

8 Cut along the central crease.

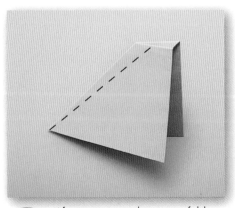

9 After cutting, inside reverse fold along the dashed line shown in the figure.

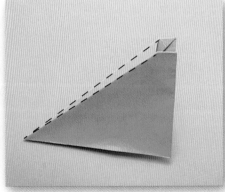

10 Inside reverse fold as shown in the figure.

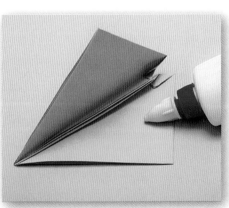

11 Use glue inside.

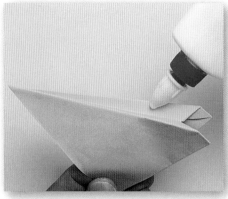

12 And use glue on the inside reverse fold part and cohere.

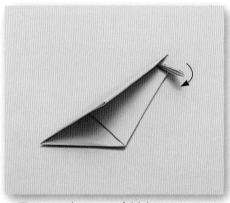

13 Done. Repeat to make two wings.

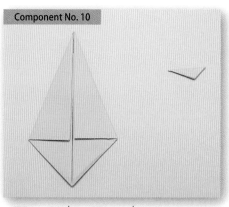

1 Make a Kite and use a square of size $1/64$ to make a Basic component eleven.

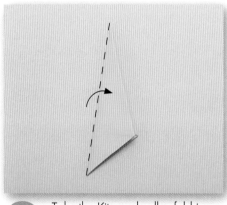

2 Take the Kite and valley fold in half along the center.

3 Inside reverse fold the top corner.

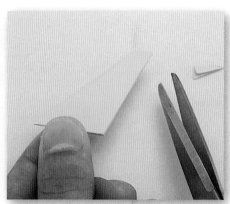

4 Cut along the edge to remove the protrusion.

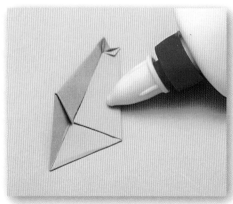

5 Use glue inside.

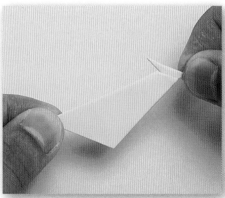

6 Glue the Basic component eleven inside as shown in the figure.

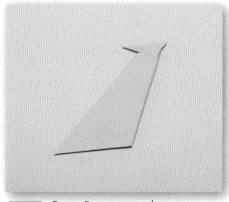

7 Done. Repeat to make two horizontal stabilizers.

Assembly Procedure

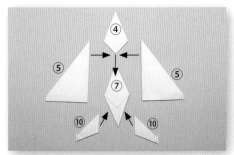

1 Use components no. 4, 5, 7, and 10 for airframe.

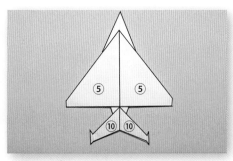

2 Glue component no. 7 to the bottom of component no. 4, and glue two components no. 5 on both sides, and glue two components no. 10 on both sides.

3 Flip over.

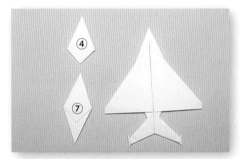

4 Then use the remaining components no. 4 and 7.

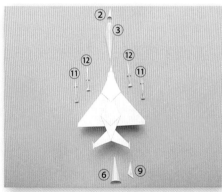

5 Glue components no. 4 and 7 to the airframe underbelly to match the top side.

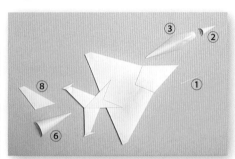

6 Use components no. 1, 2, 3, 6, and 8 for the top half.

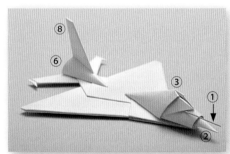

7 Component no. 3 is the nose and is glued on front of the airframe. Component no. 2 is glued into the small hole of the nose. Component no. 1 is glued on the right side of the nose. Component no. 6 is the engine and is glued to the rear of the airframe. Component no. 8 is the vertical stabilizer and is glued vertically on the engine as shown in the figure.

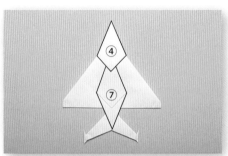

8 Then use components no. 2, 3, 6, 9, 11, and 12 for the bottom half.

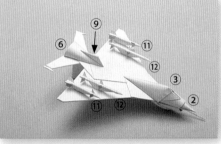

9 Component no. 3 is the nose in the front of the airframe; glue to the nose section on the top half. Component no. 2 is glued into the small hole of the nose. Component no. 6 is the engine and is glued to the rear of the airframe. Component no. 9 is glued vertically on the engine. Components no. 11 and 12 are missiles and are glued vertically on wings as shown in the figure.

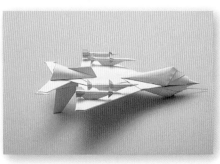

10 Reverse side.

11 Top view.

F-104
Star Fighter

Level of difficulty ★★★★☆

Specifications

Contractor: Lockheed Martin
Crew: 1
Length: 54 ft, 8 in
Wingspan: 21 ft, 9 in
Height: 13 ft, 5 in
Empty Weight: 13,380 lbs
Max. Takeoff Weight: 25,840 lbs
Speed: 1,450 mph (Mach 2.2)
Range: 730 miles

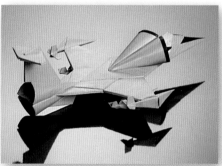

Component No.	Method
❶	Basic component nine: Nose
❷	Basic component two: Rhombus
❸	Special component: Air intake, shown as follows
❹	Special component: Wing, shown as follows
❺	Basic component eleven
❻	Basic component six: Half cone
❼	Special component: Vertical stabilizer, shown as follows
❽	Special component: Horizontal stabilizer, shown as follows
❾	Special component: Fuel tank, shown as follows
❿	Special component: Fuel tank, shown as follows

All of the components needed for assembling an F-104 Star Fighter are shown in the figure below.

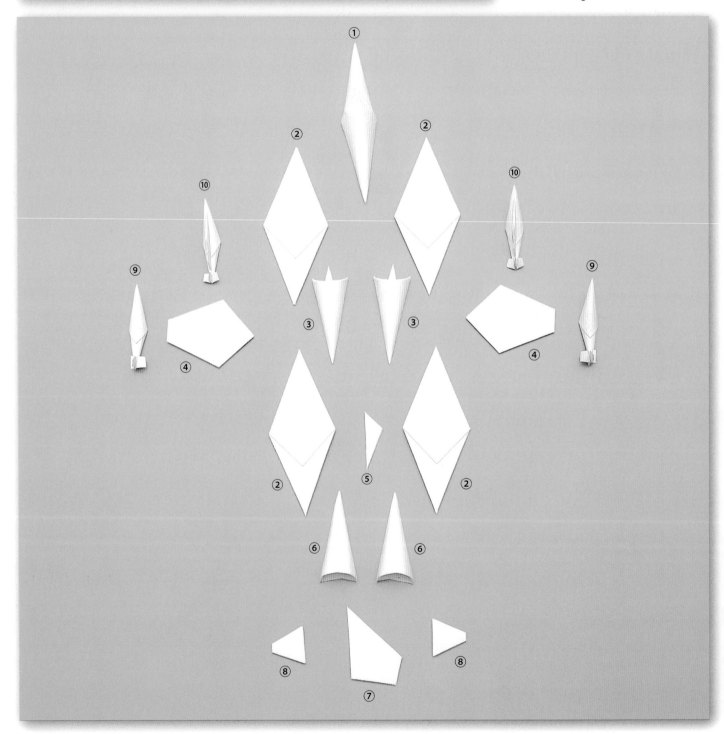

Methods for Special Components

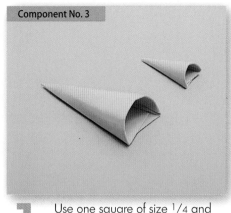

1 Use one square of size $1/4$ and one square of size $1/16$ to make two Half cones.

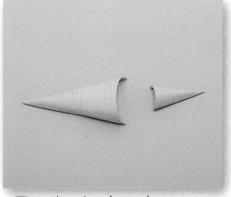

2 Place them face to face.

3 Use glue on the bottom of the small half cone, and glue it into the big half cone. Done. Repeat to make two air intakes.

Component No. 4

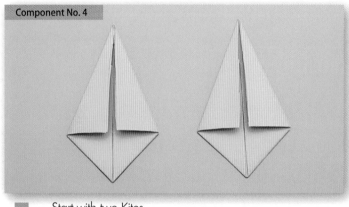

1 Start with two Kites.

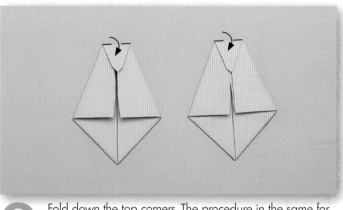

2 Fold down the top corners. The procedure in the same for the two parts.

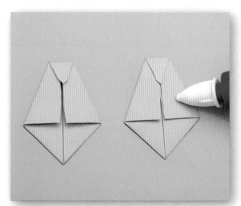

3 Use glue on one and glue the two parts to each other completely.

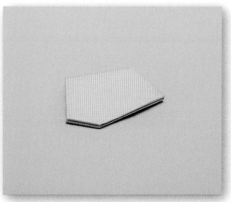

4 Done. Repeat to make two wings.

Component No. 7

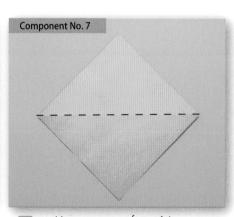

1 Use a square of size $1/4$.

2 Valley fold in half into a triangle.

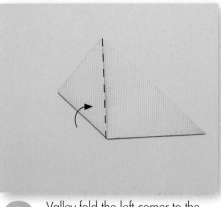

3 Valley fold the left corner to the center.

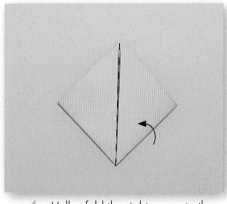

4 Valley fold the right corner to the center.

5 Valley fold in half along the center.

6 Inside reverse fold the top corner.

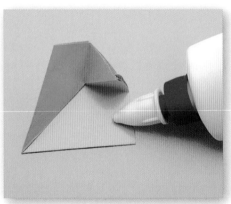

7 Use glue inside and cohere.

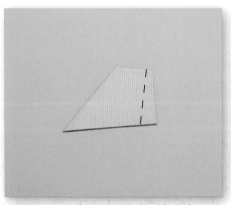

8 Cut along the dashed line shown in the figure.

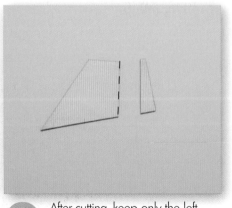

9 After cutting, keep only the left section.

10 Done.

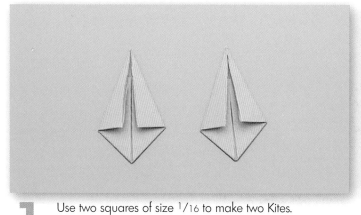

1 Use two squares of size 1/16 to make two Kites.

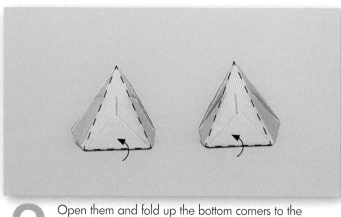

2 Open them and fold up the bottom corners to the creases. The procedure is the same for the two parts.

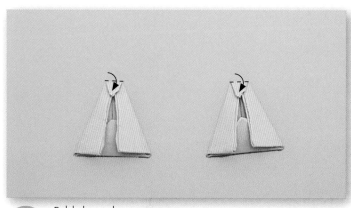

3 Fold down the top coners.

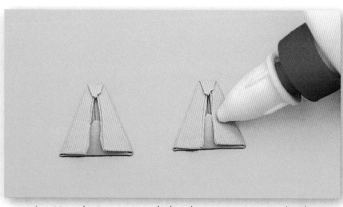

4 Use glue on one and glue the two parts to each other completely.

5 Done. Repeat to make two horizontal stabilizers.

Component No. 9

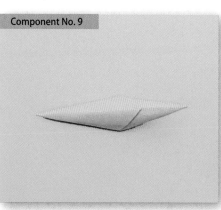

1 Start with a Basic component seventeen.

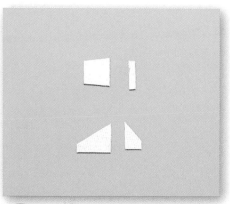

2 Cut four pieces of cardboard as shown in the figure.

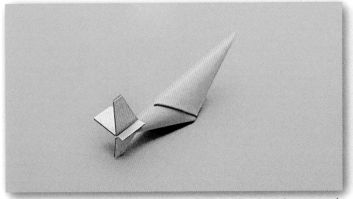

3 Glue these four pieces of paperboard at four directions of the Basic component seventeen as shown in the figure.

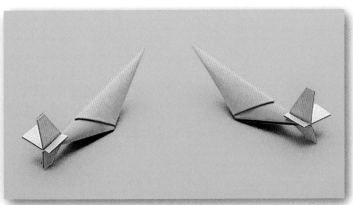

4 Done. Repeat to make two fuel tanks, but notice that the direction of these two fuel tanks is symmetrical.

Component No. 10

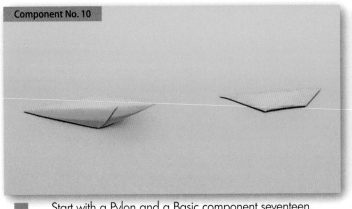

1 Start with a Pylon and a Basic component seventeen.

2 Cut three pieces of cardboard as shown in the figure.

3 Glue these three pieces of paperboard at top, right, and left of the Basic component seventeen, and glue the Pylon vertically on the Basic component seventeen as shown in the figure. Done. Repeat to make two fuel tanks.

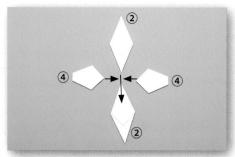

1 Use components no. 2 and 4 for airframe.

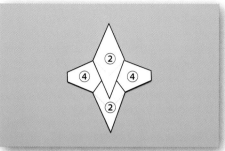

2 Glue one of components no. 2 to the bottom of another component no. 2 and glue two components no. 4 on both sides for wings.

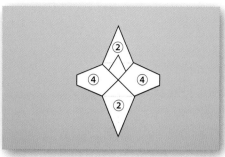

3 Flip over.

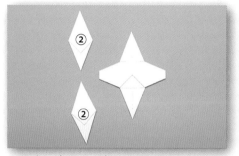

4 Then use the remaining components no. 2.

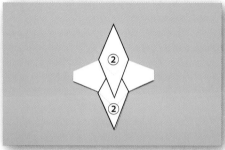

5 Glue components no. 2 to the airframe underbelly to match the top side.

6 Use components no. 1, 3, 6, 7, and 8 for the top half.

7 Component no. 1 is the nose and is glued on front of the airframe. Two components no. 3 are air intakes and are glued on both sides of the nose. Component no. 6 is glued to the rear of the airframe. Component no. 7 is glued vertically on the engine. Two components no. 8 are glued horizontally on the top section, both sides of the vertical stabilizer.

8 Then use components no. 5, 6, 9, and 10 for the bottom half.

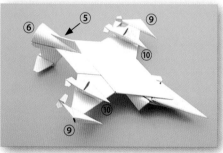

9 Component no. 6 is the engine and is glued to the rear of the airframe. Component no. 5 is glued vertically on the engine. Two components no. 9 are fuel tanks and are glued on both sides of wings. Two components no. 10 are also fuel tanks and are glued vertically on wings as shown in the figure.

10 Reverse side.

11 Top view.

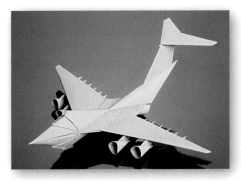

C-5
Galaxy

Specifications

Contractor: Lockheed Martin
Crew: 6
Length: 247 ft, 10 in
Wingspan: 222 ft, 9 in
Height: 65 ft
Empty Weight: 374,000 lbs
Max. Takeoff Weight: 840,000 lbs
Speed: 520 mph (Mach 0.77)

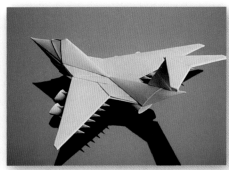

Component No. 5	Method
1	Basic component nine: Nose
2	Basic component two: Rhombus
3	Use two squares of size $^1/_4$ to make a "Basic component seventeen"
4	Basic component six: Half cone
5	Special component: Wing, shown as follows
6	Special component: Fuselage, shown as follows
7	Special component: Vertical stabilizer, shown as follows
8	Basic component ten: Horizontal stabilizer
9	Use squares of size $^1/_{64}$ to make "Basic component eleven"
10	Special component: Engine, shown as follows

All of the components needed for assembling a C-5 Galaxy are shown in the figure below.

Methods for Special Components

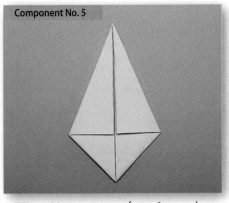

1 Use a square of size 1 to make a Kite.

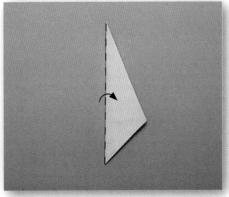

2 Valley fold in half along the center.

3 Inside reverse fold the top corner.

4 Cut along the edge to remove the protrusion.

5 Use glue inside and cohere.

6 Done. Repeat to make two wings.

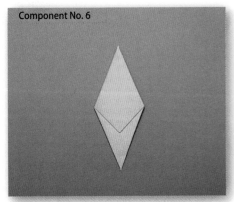

1 Start with a Rhombus.

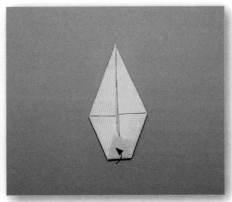

2 Flip over and fold up the bottom corner.

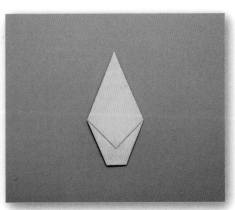

3 Flip over and it's done. Repeat to make two Fuselages.

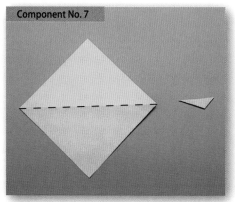

1 Use a square of size ¹/4 and a Basic component eleven.

2 Start with the square of size ¹/4 and valley fold in half into a triangle.

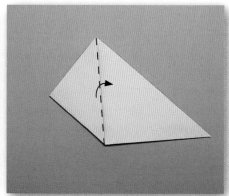

3 Valley fold the left corner to the center.

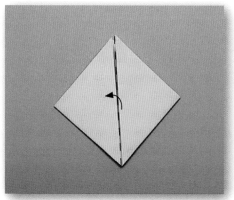

4 Valley fold the right corner to the center.

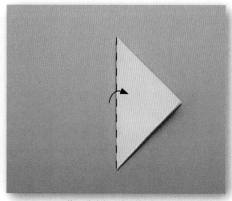

5 Valley fold in half along the center.

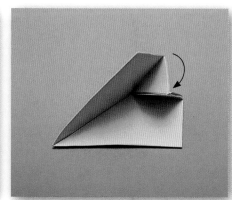

6 Inside reverse fold the top corner.

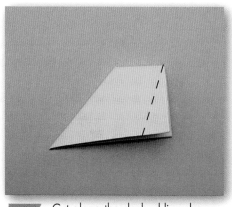

7 Cut along the dashed line shown in the figure.

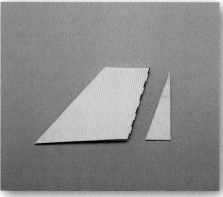

8 After cutting, keep only the left section.

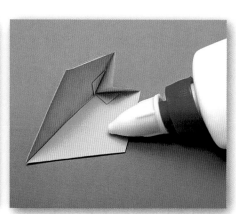

9 Use glue inside.

10 Glue the Basic component eleven inside the top section of the vertical stabilizer.

11 Done.

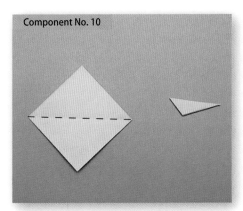

1 Start with a square of size 1/16 and a Basic component eleven.

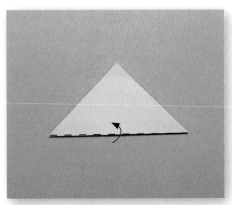

2 Take the square of size 1/16 and valley fold in half into a triangle.

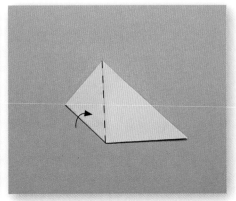

3 Valley fold the left corner to the center.

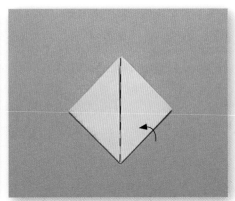

4 Valley fold the right corner to the center.

5 Cut off the two corners on the top layer for convenience in later steps. The cut parts will not be visible on the exterior.

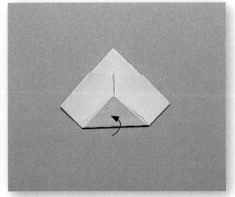

6 Fold up the bottom corner to the center.

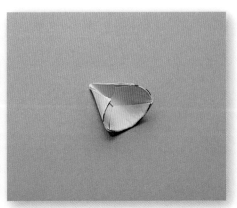

7 Curl the edge to a curve along the dashed line shown in the figure.

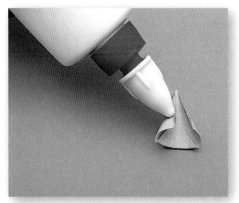

8 Use glue on the edge.

9 Cohere. The first part is complete.

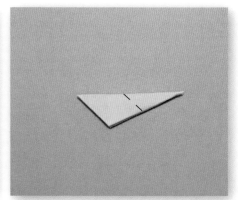

10 Then cut the Basic component eleven into two sections along the dashed line shown in the figure.

11 After cutting, keep only the left section and discard the right section.

12 The second part is complete.

13 Use glue on the edge of the second part and cohere vertically to the first part shown in the figure. Repeat three times to make four engines total.

Assembly Procedure

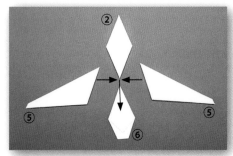

1 Use components no. 2, 5, and 6 for the airframe.

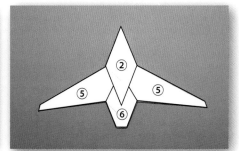

2 Glue component no. 6 to the bottom of component no. 2, and glue two components no. 5 on both sides for wings as shown in the figure.

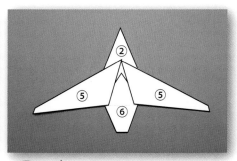

3 Flip over.

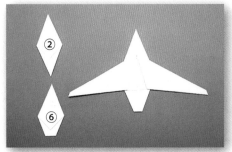

4 Then use the remaining components no. 2 and 6.

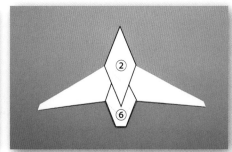

5 Glue components no. 2 and 6 to the airframe underbelly to match the top side.

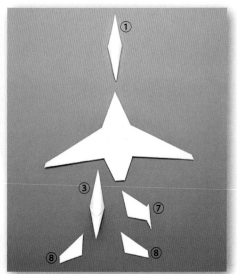

6 Use components no. 1, 3, 7, and 8 for the top half.

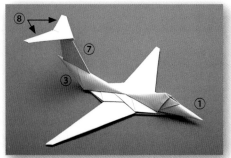

7 Component no. 1 is glued on the front of the airframe. Component no. 3 is glued to the rear of the airframe. Component no. 7 is glued vertically on the top of component no. 3. Two components no. 8 make up the horizontal stabilizer and are glued horizontally on the vertical stabilizer.

8 Use components no. 1, 4, 9, and 10 for the bottom half.

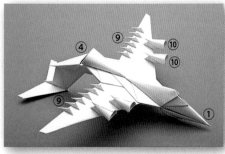

9 Component no. 1 is the nose in the front of the airframe; glue to the nose section on the top half. Component no. 4 is glued in the rear of the airframe. The anti-shock bodies, twelve components no. 9, are glued vertically on wings trailing edge. The four components no.10 are engines, and are glued vertically on wings as shown in the figure

10

11 Reverse side.

Top view.

E-2
Hawkeye

Level of difficulty ★★★★★

Specifications

Contractor: Grumann
Crew: 5
Length: 57 ft, 6 in
Wingspan: 80 ft, 7 in
Height: 18 ft, 3 in
Empty Weight: 38,060 lbs
Max. Takeoff Weight: 51,930 lbs
Range: 350 miles

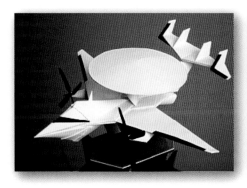

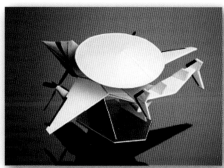

Component No.	Method
❶	Basic component nine: Nose
❷	Basic component two: Rhombus
❸	Special component, shown as follows
❹	Special component: Fuselage, shown as follows
❺	Basic component six: Half cone
❻	Special component: Wing, shown as follows
❼	Special component: Fuselage, shown as follows
❽	Special component: Stabilizer, shown as follows
❾	Special component: Radar, shown as follows
❿	Special component: Propeller, shown as follows

All of the components needed for assembling an E-2 Hawkeye are shown in the figure below.

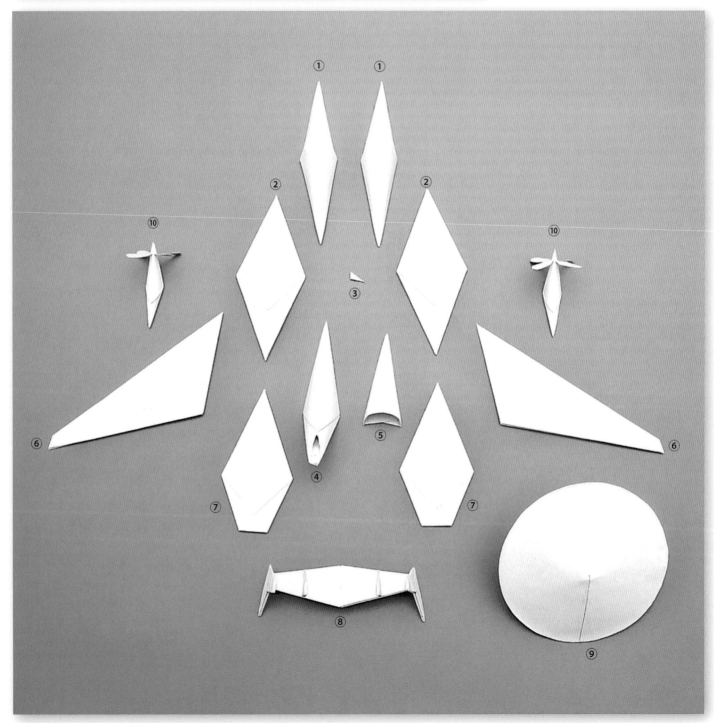

Methods for Special Components

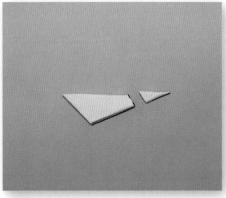

1 Start with a Basic component eleven and cut it into two sections along the dashed line shown in the figure.

2 After cutting, keep only the triangle in the right section and discard the left section.

3 Done.

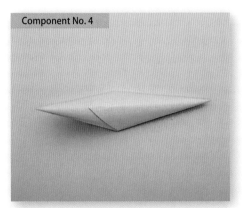

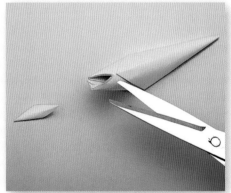

1 Use two squares of size $1/4$ to make a Basic component seventeen.

2 Cut off the tail corner horizontally as shown in the figure.

3 Done.

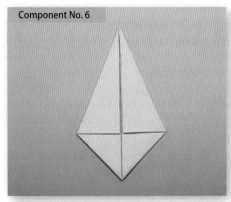

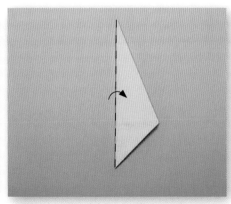

1 Use a square of size 1 to make a Kite.

2 Valley fold in half along the center.

3 Inside reverse fold the top corner.

4 Cut along the edge to remove the protrusion.

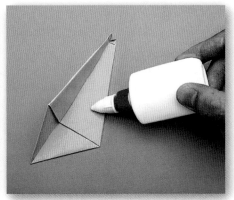

5 Use glue inside and cohere.

6 Done. Repeat to make two wings.

Component No. 7

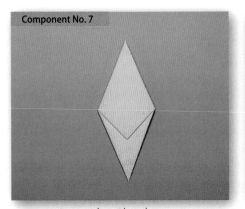

1 Start with a Rhombus.

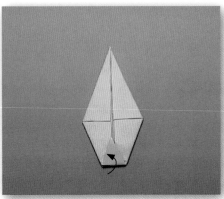

2 Flip over and fold up the bottom corner.

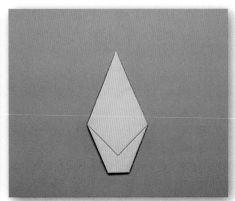

3 Flip over and it's done. Repeat to make two fuselages.

Component No. 8

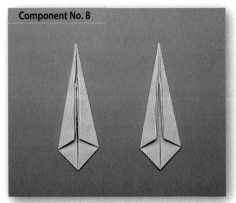

1 Start with two Basic components five.

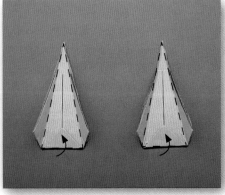

2 Open them and fold up the bottom corners to the creases. The procedure is the same for the two parts.

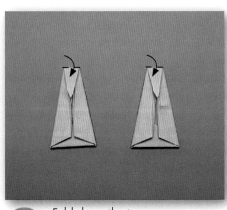

3 Fold down the top corners.

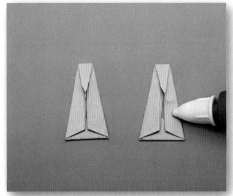

4 Use glue on one part.

5 Glue two parts to each other completely.

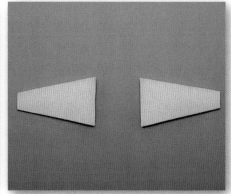

6 Repeat to make two of these components and place them face to face.

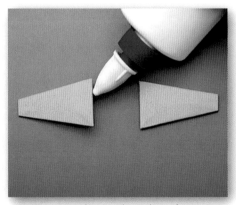

7 Use glue on the edge of one component.

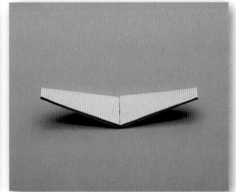

8 Glue two components to each other. Notice that, they are not horizontal but with an angle as shown in the figure. The first part is complete.

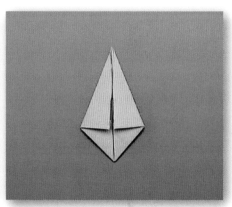

9 Then use a square of size $1/16$ to make a Kite.

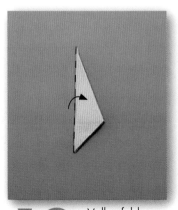

10 Valley fold in half along the center.

11 Inside reverse fold the top corner.

12 Cut along the edge to remove the protrusion.

13 Use glue inside and cohere.

14 The second part is complete. Repeat to make two these components.

15 Then use a square of size 1/16 to make a Kite.

16 Valley fold in half along the center.

17 Inside reverse fold the top corner.

18 Cut along the edge to remove the protrusion.

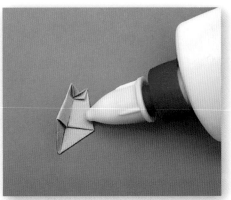

19 Use glue inside and cohere.

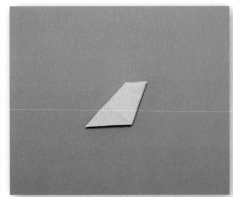

20 The third part is complete. Repeat three times to make four of these components total.

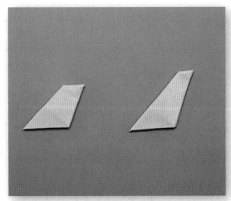

21 Compare the second part with the third part. The difference between them is that one has less inside reverse fold and the other has more inside reverse fold, so one is longer and one is shorter.

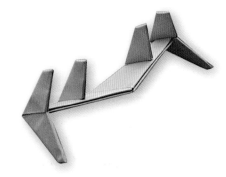

22 Glue two second parts and four third parts to the first part as shown in the figure and it's done.

Component No. 9

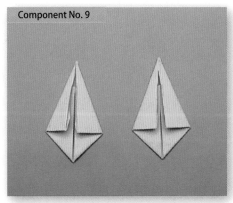

1 Use two squares of size 1/16 to make two Kites.

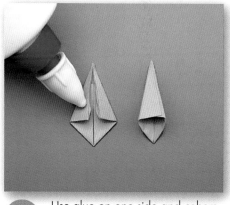

2 Use glue on one side and cohere.

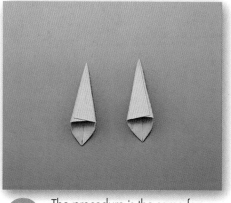

3 The procedure is the same for the two parts.

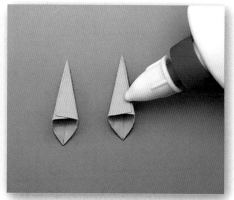

4 Use glue on one and glue the two parts to each other completely.

5 The first part is complete.

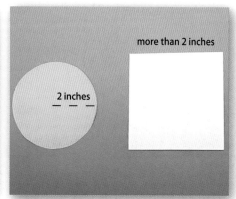

6 Use a circle of 2 inch radius and a cardboard square more than 2 inches long.

7 Cut the round shape along the radius.

8 Use glue on the edge.

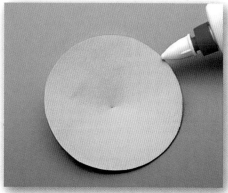

9 Glue the edges to make a cone, then use glue on the edge of the cone.

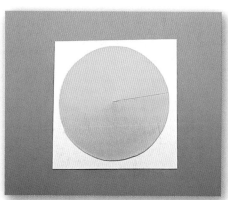

10 Glue to the cardboard square.

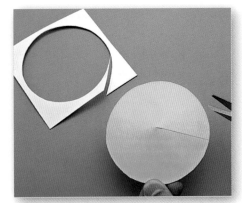

11 Cut along the edge of the cone.

12 Flip over and cut a small aperture on the center.

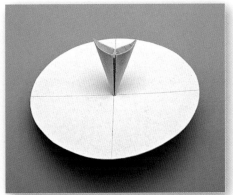

13 Glue the first part to the aperture as shown in the figure.

14 Done.

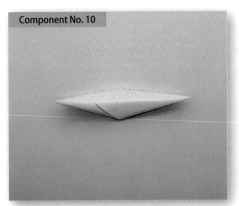

Component No. 10

1 Use a Basic component seventeen.

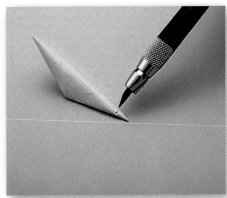

2 Cut two small chinks on the peak.

3 Similarly, cut two small chinks on the peak in the back side.

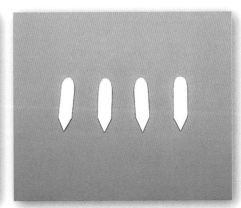

4 Cut four propellers using cardboard as shown in figure.

5 Use glue on the tips of the four propellers and cohere into the four chinks on the peak as shown in the figure and it's done. Repeat to make two propellers.

Assembly Procedure

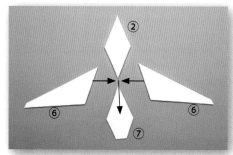

1 Use components no. 2, 6, and 7 for the airframe.

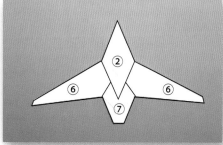

2 Glue component no. 7 to the bottom of component no. 2, and glue two components no. 6 on both sides for wings.

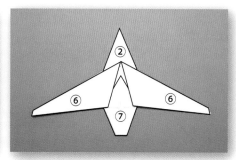

3 Flip over.

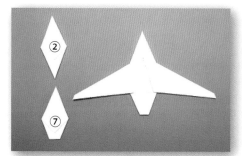

4 Then use the remaining components no. 2 and 7.

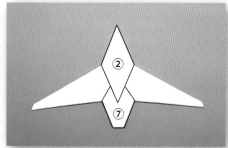

5 Glue components no. 2 and 7 to the airframe underbelly to match the top side.

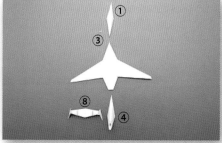

6 Use components no. 1, 3, 4, and 8 for the top half.

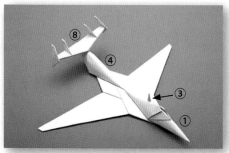

7 Component no. 1 is the nose and is glued on the front of the airframe. Component no. 3 is glued vertically on the nose. Component no. 4 is glued to the rear of the airframe. Component no. 8 is the stabilizer and is glued on the top of component no. 4 as shown in the figure.

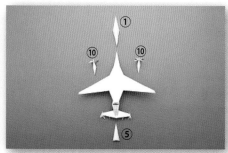

8 Then use components no. 1, 5, and 10 for the bottom half.

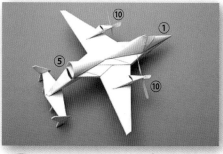

9 Component no. 1 is the nose in the front of the airframe; glue to the nose section on the top half. Component no. 5 is glued to the rear of the airframe. Two components no. 10 are propellers and are glued on wings.

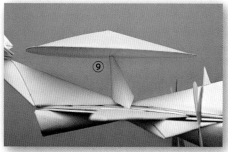

10 Finally, component no. 9 is the radar and is glued vertically to the center on the top half as shown in the figure.

11 Top view.

A-10
Thunderbolt II

Level of difficulty ★★★★★

Specifications

Contractor: Fairchild
Crew: 1
Length: 53 ft, 4 in
Wingspan: 57 ft, 6 in
Height: 14 ft, 8 in
Empty Weight: 25,600 lbs
Max. Takeoff Weight: 51,000 lbs
Speed: 420 mph (Mach 0.56)
Range: 800 miles

Component No.	Method
❶	Basic component nine: Nose
❷	Basic component twelve
❸	Special component, shown as follows
❹	Basic component two: Rhombus
❺	Special component: Fuselage, shown as follows
❻	Basic component six: Half cone
❼	Special component: Wing, shown as follows
❽	Special component: Fuselage, shown as follows
❾	Special component: Engine, shown as follows
❿	Special component: Stabilizer, shown as follows
⓫	Special component: Missile set, shown as follows
⓬	Basic component sixteen: The combination of missile no. 3 and pylon
⓭	Basic component seventeen

All of the components needed for assembling an A-10 Thunderbolt II are shown in the figure below.

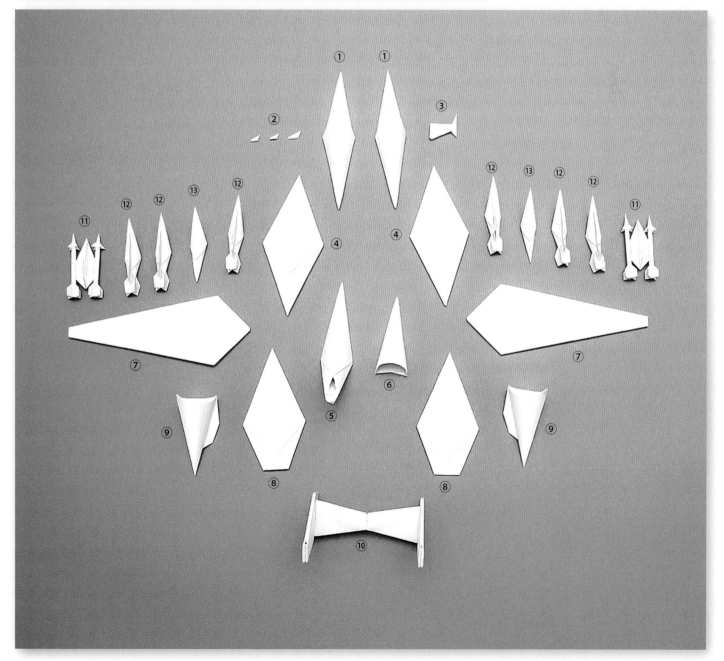

Methods for Special Components

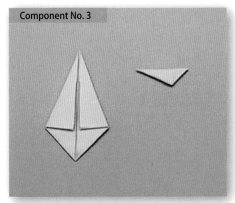

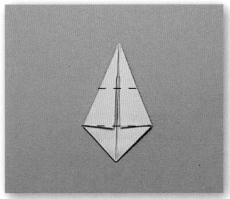

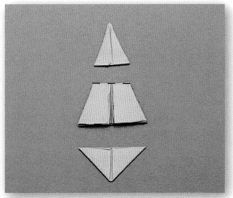

1 Use a square of size ¹/16 to make a Kite and use a square of size ¹/64 to make a Basic component eleven.

2 Start with the Kite and cut it into three sections along the dashed lines shown in the figure.

3 After cutting, keep only the trapezoid (the middle section) and discard the others.

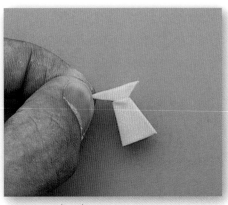

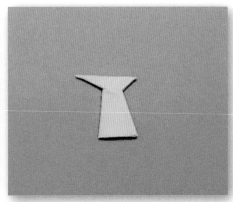

4 Use glue inside.

5 Glue the Basic component eleven inside the top section.

6 Done.

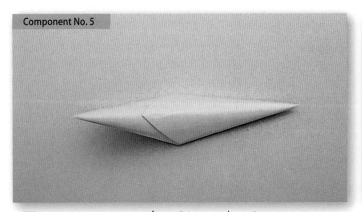

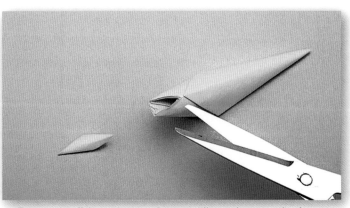

1 Use two squares of size ¹/4 to make a Basic component seventeen.

2 Cut off the tail corner horizontally as shown in the figure.

3 Done.

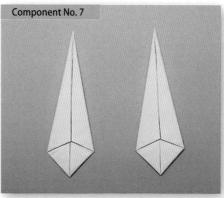

1 Use two squares of size 1 to make two Basic components five.

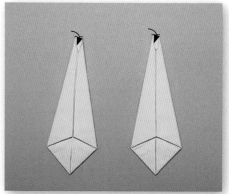

2 Fold down the top corner. The procedure is the same for the two parts.

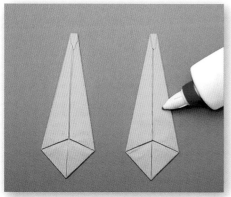

3 Use glue on one and glue the two parts to each other completely.

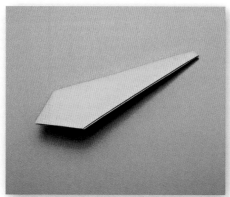

4 Done. Repeat to make two wings.

1 Start with a Rhombus.

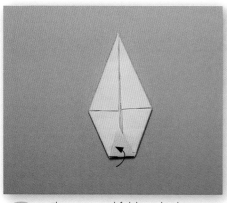

2 Flip over and fold up the bottom corner.

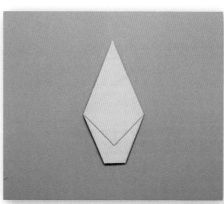

3 Flip over and it's done. Repeat to make two Fuselages.

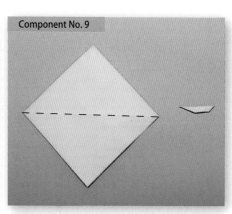

1 Use a square of size $1/4$ and a Pylon.

2 Start with the square of size $1/4$ and valley fold in half into a triangle.

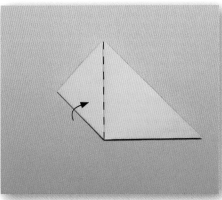

3 Valley fold the left corner to the center.

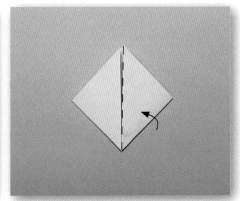

4 Valley fold the right corner to the center.

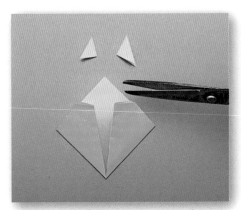

5 Cut off the two corners on the top layer for convenience in later steps. The cut parts will not be visible on the exterior.

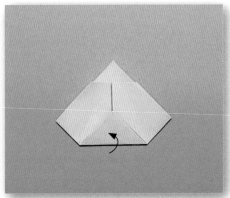

6 Fold up the bottom corner to the center.

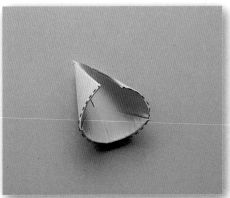

7 Curl the edge to a curve along the dashed line shown in the figure.

8 Use glue on the edge.

9 Cohere. The first part is complete.

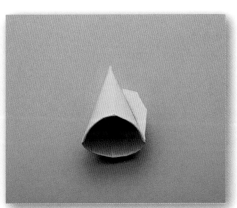

10 Use glue on the edge of the Pylon, vertically glue to the completed first part and it's done.

11 Repeat to make two engines, but notice that the direction of these two components is symmetrical.

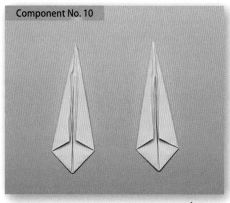

1 Use two Basic components five.

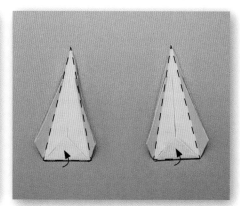

2 Open them and fold up the bottom corners to the creases. The procedure is the same for the two parts.

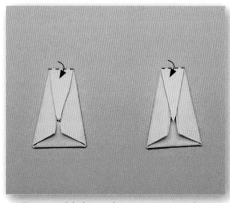

3 Fold down the top corners. The procedure is the same for the two parts.

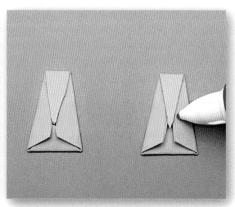

4 Use glue on one part.

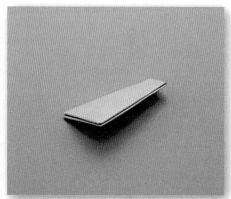

5 Glue the two parts to each other completely.

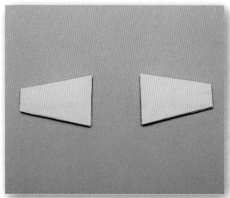

6 Repeat to make two of these components and place them face to face.

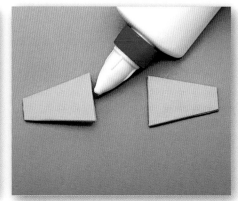

7 Use glue on the edge of one component.

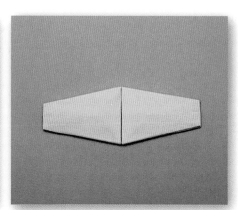

8 Glue two components to each other. The first part is complete.

A-10 Thunderbolt II   **153**

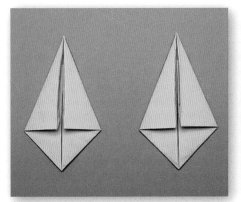

9 Then use the two Kites.

10 Use one and open it. Valley fold the right edge to the left crease.

11 Use glue inside.

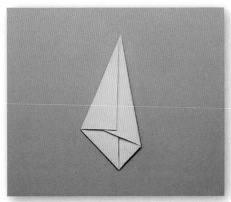

12 Cohere.

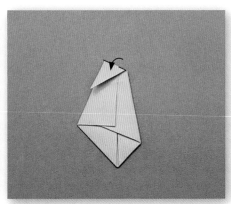

13 Fold down the top corner.

14 Use the other and open it. Valley fold the left edge to the right crease.

15 Use glue inside.

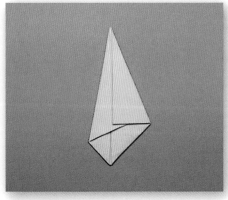

16 Cohere.

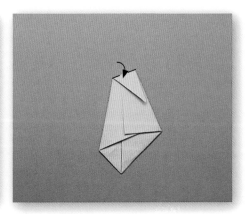

17 Fold down the top corner.

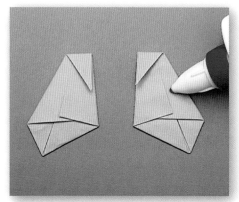

18 After completing both components, use glue on one of them.

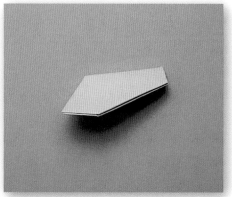

19 Glue two components to each other completely.

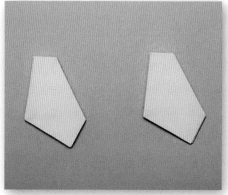

20 Repeat to make two of these components. The second part is complete.

21 Glue the second part to both sides of the first part as shown in the figure and it's done.

Component No. 11

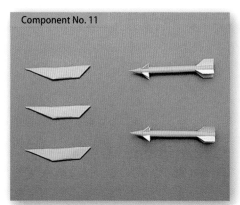

1 Start with three Pylons and two of Missile no. 1

2 Start with the three Pylons and use glue on the edge of each Pylon, so that you can glue them vertically as shown in the figure.

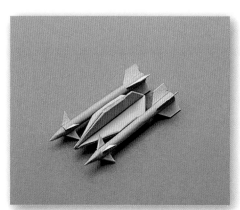

3 Then glue two missiles to both sides of the pylon as shown in the figure and it's done. Repeat to make two missile sets.

Assembly Procedure

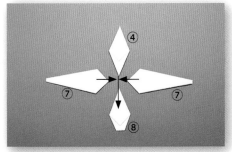

1 Use components no. 4, 7, and 8 for the airframe.

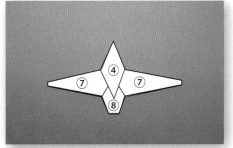

2 Glue component no. 8 to the bottom of component no. 4, and glue two components no. 7 on both sides for wings as shown in the figure.

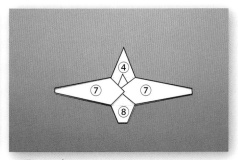

3 Flip over.

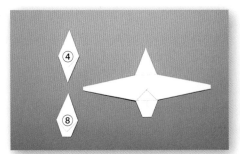

4 Then use the remaining components no. 4 and 8.

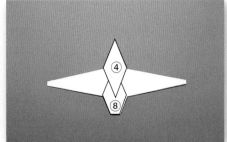

5 Glue components no. 4 and 8 to the airframe underbelly to match the top side.

6 Use components no. 1, 2, 5, 9, and 10 for the top half.

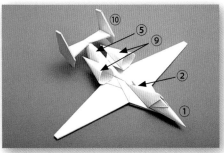

7 Component no. 1 is glued on the front of the airframe. Component no. 2 is glued in the rear of the nose vertically. Component no. 5 is glued to the rear of the airframe. Two components no. 9 are glued horizontally on both sides of component no. 5. Component no. 10 is glued on the top of component no. 5.

8 Then use components no.1, 2, 3, 6, 11, 12, and 13 for the bottom half.

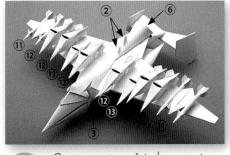

9 Component no. 1 is the nose in the front of the airframe; glue to the nose section on the top half. Component no. 6 is glued in the rear of the airframe. Two components no. 2 are glued vertically on component no. 6. Component no. 3 is glued vertically on the left of the nose. Two components no. 13 are glued on wings. Components no. 11 and 12 are missiles and are glued on wings as shown in the figure.

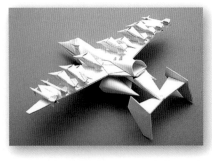

10 Reverse side.

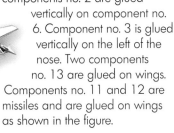

11 Top view.

Works

Here are a few sample planes in action photos to inspire your folding!

About the Author

Patrick Wang currently majors in Electrical Engineering doctoral degree at University of Houston, Houston, Texas.

Since I was a child, I was very interested in airplanes. My father was an air force pilot and I dreamed of being an excellent fighter pilot as well—maybe I inherited his flying dreams. As I got older, I was more and more interested in airplane models. I bought lots of plastic airplane models, and I am still proud of every well-made model in my showcase.

However, I always felt that those plastic models took too much money and time before I could display them. Therefore, I started utilizing the materials around me, with easier steps and cheaper ways to make these origami airplanes which even surprised myself. "Amazing" is the first word from mouths when these origami airplanes are shown to people. I believe that, by following the steps in this book with a little patience, you can make your own amazing Origami Model Airplanes as well.

Patrick Wang

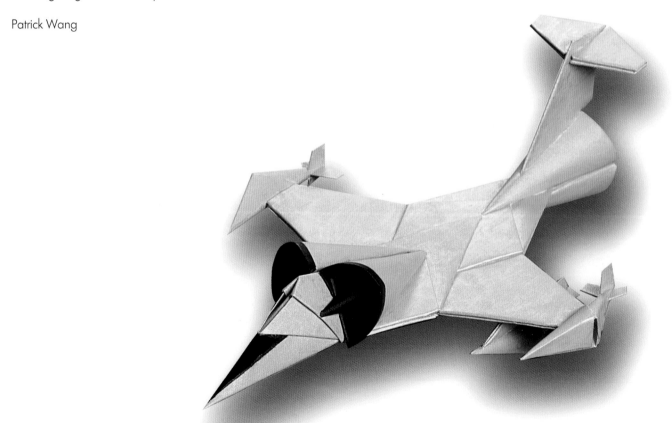